ACCOUNTABILITY IN NAMIBIA

Human Rights and the Transition to Democracy

August 1992

An Africa Watch Report

A Division of Human Rights Watch

485 Fifth Avenue
New York, NY 10017-6104
Tel: (212) 972-8400
Fax: (212) 972-0905

90 Borough High Street
London SE1 1LL, U.K.
Tel: (071) 378-8029
Fax: (071) 378-8008

1522 K Street, NW, Suite 910
Washington, DC 20005-1202
Tel: (202) 371-6592
Fax: (202) 371-0124

ISBN 1-56432-117-7

HUMAN RIGHTS WATCH

Human Rights Watch conducts regular, systematic investigations of human rights abuses in some seventy countries around the world. It addresses the human rights practices of governments of all political stripes, of all geopolitical alignments, and of all ethnic and religious persuasions. In internal wars it documents violations by both governments and rebel groups. Human Rights Watch defends freedom of thought and expression, due process and equal protection of the law; it documents and denounces murders, disappearances, torture, arbitrary imprisonment, exile, censorship and other abuses of internationally recognized human rights.

Human Rights Watch began in 1978 with the founding of its Helsinki division. Today, it includes five divisions covering Africa, the Americas, Asia, the Middle East, as well as the signatories of the Helsinki accords. It also includes five collaborative projects on arms transfers, children's rights, free expression, prison conditions, and women's rights. It maintains offices in New York, Washington, Los Angeles, London, Brussels, Moscow, Belgrade, Zagreb, Dushanbe, and Hong Kong. Human Rights Watch is an independent, nongovernmental organization, supported by contributions from private individuals and foundations worldwide. It accepts no government funds, directly or indirectly.

The staff includes Kenneth Roth, executive director; Cynthia Brown, program director; Holly J. Burkhalter, advocacy director; Gara LaMarche, associate director; Juan Méndez, general counsel; Susan Osnos, communications director; and Derrick Wong, finance and administration director.

The regional directors of Human Rights Watch are Abdullahi An-Na'im, Africa; José Miguel Vivanco, Americas; Sidney Jones, Asia; Jeri Laber, Helsinki; and Christopher E. George, Middle East. The project directors are Stephen Goose (acting), Arms Project; Lois Whitman, Children's Rights Project; Gara LaMarche, Free Expression Project; Joanna Weschler, Prison Project; and Dorothy Q. Thomas, Women's Rights Project.

The members of the board of directors are Robert L. Bernstein, chair; Adrian W. DeWind, vice chair; Roland Algrant, Lisa Anderson, Peter D. Bell, Alice L. Brown, William Carmichael, Dorothy Cullman, Irene Diamond, Edith Everett, Jonathan Fanton, Alan Finberg, Jack Greenberg, Alice H. Henkin, Harold Hongju Koh, Stephen L. Kass, Marina Pinto Kaufman, Alexander MacGregor, Josh Mailman, Peter Osnos, Kathleen Peratis, Bruce Rabb, Orville Schell, Gary G. Sick, Malcolm Smith, Nahid Toubia, Maureen White, and Rosalind C. Whitehead.

Addresses for Human Rights Watch
485 Fifth Avenue, New York, NY 10017-6104
Tel: (212) 972-8400, Fax: (212) 972-0905, E-mail: hrwatchnyc@igc.apc.org

1522 K Street, N.W., #910, Washington, DC 20005-1202
Tel: (202) 371-6592, Fax: (202) 371-0124, E-mail: hrwatchdc@igc.apc.org

10951 West Pico Blvd., #203, Los Angeles, CA 90064-2126
Tel: (310) 475-3070, Fax: (310) 475-5613, E-mail: hrwatchla@igc.apc.org

33 Islington High Street, N1 9LH London, UK
Tel: (71) 713-1995, Fax: (71) 713-1800, E-mail: hrwatchuk@gn.apc.org

15 Rue Van Campenhout, 1040 Brussels, Belgium
Tel: (2) 732-2009, Fax: (2) 732-0471, E-mail: hrwatcheu@gn.apc.org

TABLE OF CONTENTS

ABBREVIATIONS AND GLOSSARY . . . . page i

ACKNOWLEDGMENTS iii

NOTE ON THE TEXT iv

MAP v

1. INTRODUCTION 1

2. GERMAN AND SOUTH AFRICAN COLONIAL RULE 8
   German Colonial Conquest 8
   South African Colonial Rule 11
   Governance, Land and Grand Apartheid 13

3. BACKGROUND TO THE WAR 17
   South African Forces 17
      SADF and SWATF 17
      Koevoet 17
      Security Police 19
      Homeguards 20
   SWAPO Military Forces 20
   The Course of the War 21
      Security Legislation 22
      The 1980s 23

4. THE BOMBING OF REFUGEE CAMPS AND DETENTIONS AT MARIENTAL . . 27
   Introduction 27
   Assault on the Camps 27
   Detentions at Mariental 32

5. VIOLENCE AGAINST THE CIVILIAN POPULATION OF THE NORTH 38
   Legal Standards 38
   Arbitrary Arrests 39
   Interrogation and Torture 43
   Disappearances 56
   Bombings 62

6. ACCOUNTABILITY FOR SOUTH AFRICAN ABUSES 64
   Executive Amnesties 64
   Appointment of Officers from the South African Colonial Regime 65

7. INTRODUCTION TO SWAPO ABUSES 68
    Legal Standards 71
    Interrogation and Torture 72
    The Dungeons 79
    Conditions in the Dungeons 82
    Physical Abuse 85
    Deaths 85
    Transfers and Disappearances 87
    Women Detainees 88
    Pregnancy and Childbearing in the Dungeon 90
    Children 91

8. THE RELEASE OF SWAPO DETAINEES 92
    The Release of the 210—May 24, 1989 93

9. THE UNITED NATIONS MISSION ON DETAINEES 98
    Specific Findings 100
    Lack of Independence 102

10. RESPONSIBILITY FOR SWAPO ABUSES 104
    The Hawala Appointment 108

10. INVESTIGATIONS AFTER INDEPENDENCE 111

RECOMMENDATIONS 117

APPENDIX 1: Human Rights Watch Policy
    on Accountability for Past Human Rights Auses 119

ABBREVIATIONS AND GLOSSARY

Casspirs — Armored personel carriers used by the South African forces.

CNN — Council of Churches in Namibia

Cuca Shop — A general dealer's store that doubles as a pub.

FAPLA — Forças Armadas Para a Libertação de Angola, the Angolan government's armed forces.

ICRC — International Committee of the Red Cross

KMRC — Karl Marx Reception Center

knoberries — Wooden stick-like clubs.

Koevoet — A South African para-military unit.

Kraal — The traditional Ovambo homestead.

Makukunya — An Oshivambo term for bloodsuckers that refered to Koevoet members.

MPLA — Movimento Popular de Libertação de Angola, the Angolan government.

pangas — Machetes

PC — Parents' Committee

PCC — Political Consultative Committee

PLAN — People's Liberation Army of Namibia

SADF — South African Defence Forces

sjamboks — Hippo-hide whips.

SRSG — Special Representative of the United Nations Secretary-General

SWAPO — South West African People's Organization

SWATF — South West Africa Territorial Force

UNHCR — United Nations High Commission for Refugees

UNITA —   União Nacional para a Independência Total de Angola, oppostition guerrilla forces in Angola.

UNMD —   United Nations Mission on Detainees

UNTAG —   United Nations Transition Assistance Group

ACKNOWLEDGMENTS

This report was written by Richard Dicker, a lawyer, who was the Orville Schell Fellow for Africa Watch in 1990-1991. He traveled to Namibia in April 1991 to conduct research and interviews. It was edited by Aryeh Neier, executive director of Human Rights Watch. Rakiya Omaar, executive director of Africa Watch, provided valuable editorial comments. Barbara Baker and Ben Penglase, Africa Watch associates, lent their technical expertise and interest.

Africa Watch is especially grateful to the many Namibians who shared their experiences, often painful ones, as well as their ideas and assessments. They spoke in the faith that this story would be told. Without their contribution, this report would not have been possible.

Africa Watch also wishes to thank those longtime supporters of Namibian independence in the United States whose advice and encouragement helped this effort come to fruition.

NOTE ON THE TEXT

The interviews with former SWAPO detainees, with one exception, were conducted in Windhoek and Katutura in April 1991. Those interviewed wished their identity to remain anonymous. Pursuant to its usual practice, Africa Watch respected the desire for confidentiality. Thus, those interviews are not footnoted in the text. In some places aliases are used for the purpose of clarity. This is indicated in the footnotes.

In the text, noms de guerre appear in quotations.

1. INTRODUCTION

When a country moves from repression to a more democratic system that respects human rights, the abuses committed under the previous regime are not forgotten by the victims, their families and their friends. It is important to them and to the society of which they are a part that there should be a day of reckoning for the terrible suffering that has been inflicted on them. Democratically elected governments in many countries, from Latin America to Eastern and Central Europe to East Asia, have had to deal with the difficult question of accountability for past abuses. Inevitably, this question has also arisen in Africa. In Uganda, the government of President Yoweri Museveni established a Commission of Inquiry to document the crimes of the regimes of Idi Amin and Milton Obote. In Ethiopia, the Transitional Government led by Meles Zenawi is just beginning to examine the violations of the Mengistu era. Other governments now undergoing transitions, including South Africa, Angola and Mozambique are likely to confront the need.

Namibia presents a complex and compelling case for accountability. The country's transition to independence and democracy was long and bloody. In 1966, after nearly seventy years of South African colonial rule, an armed struggle for independence began along the country's northern border. By the late 1970s, the South African Defence Force (SADF) had deployed large numbers of troops in the region to prevent infiltration by members of the South West Africa People's Organization (SWAPO) and its military wing, the People's Liberation Army of Namibia (PLAN), which was based in camps in southern Angola and Zambia. In addition to the SADF, the South African Ministry of Defence recruited military and para-military forces locally to stem infiltration and deter support for SWAPO among the civilian population. During the counter-insurgency war, the South African forces committed gross violations of the laws of war (also known as international humanitarian law), these included: arbitrary arrests of suspected SWAPO supporters; torture during interrogation; "disappearances" of some of those held in custody; summary executions of civilians; and rape. A few South African colonial personnel were prosecuted for such violations, but South African State President P.W. Botha intervened to halt the proceedings. He invoked a provision of South African law that indemnifies official personnel from prosecution. The handful of cases in which prosecutions were not interrupted and convictions resulted most frequently involved drunken conduct by low level military personnel.

SWAPO also engaged in a pattern of violations of the laws of war against its own members. Starting in the early 1980s, some members of SWAPO living in exile were arrested by the SWAPO/PLAN security service and accused of being South African spies. Africa Watch found that the majority of the victims were young, non-Ovambo members from the south and center of Namibia. Following arrest, they were transferred to an interrogation center at SWAPO's military headquarters in Lubango, in southwestern Angola. There, they were tortured until they confessed to working for the colonial regime and gave the names of other SWAPO traitors. The practice was neither to confront them with evidence nor to charge them with specific acts of espionage. They were then transferred to "dungeons"—pits dug into the ground where they were held under degrading and cruel conditions. Such prisoners were transferred from one camp to another without explanation; many disappeared, and have never been seen again. Others died of disease or malnutrition. According to testimony obtained by Africa Watch, SWAPO's leader,

Sam Nujoma, now President of the Republic of Namibia, visited the camps and addressed the detainees. One former detainee told us:

> May 1986 was the first visit of Sam Nujoma. The second visit of Sam Nujoma was in April 1988. Every time he came we would tell him the procedure, the scars. He was still on the side of "his sons." He was believing them. Why don't you investigate the cases, we said. He said, "You were sent by the Boers and you will stay there until the time that we liberate Namibia and we take you to your parents. We will take you to Freedom Square and you will be judged by the people of Namibia."

The armed conflict in Namibia ended after fifteen years of negotiations sponsored by the United Nations. In 1976, the UN Security Council unanimously adopted Resolution 385 which called on South Africa to withdraw from Namibia and allow free elections. The following year, South Africa and SWAPO agreed that the five Western nations then on the Security Council—the United States, France, United Kingdom, West Germany and Canada—would serve as mediators to negotiate an internationally acceptable solution. In 1978, the UN adopted Resolution 435, providing for internationally supervised elections. Resolution 435 also restated the need to end "South Africa's illegal administration of Namibia and transfer power to the people of Namibia with the assistance of the United Nations in accordance with resolution 385."

Resolution 435 also established a United Nations Transition Assistance Group (UNTAG) to be deployed for twelve months to assist the Secretary-General's Special Representative (SGSR) in ensuring the early independence of Namibia through "free and fair elections under the supervision and control of the United Nations."

In the early 1980s the implementation of Resolution 435 stalled. In 1981, the US had introduced "linkage" between the withdrawal of Cuban troops from Angola and the departure of South African forces from Namibia. In 1982, eight additional points were added to Resolution 435 by Security Council members. These included constitutional guarantees for a Bill of Rights, multi-party democracy and an independent judiciary.

In December 1988, the Brazzaville Protocol was signed. It set April 1, 1989, as the date for implementation of Resolution 435. To prepare, UNTAG personnel began to arrive in Namibia in January 1989. As the date for implementation drew close, SWAPO announced a policy of "national reconciliation" to heal the divisive wounds caused by the independence struggle. On April 1, 1989, a large scale movement of PLAN fighters into northern Namibia provoked widespread fighting in which many PLAN combatants were killed. Implementation of Resolution 435 was suspended until May 1989.

Security Council Resolution 435 required the release of political prisoners held by both sides. Though both the South Africans and SWAPO released prisoners, they were not obligated to account for those who had disappeared, or to publish information on the total number of those held. Neither side furnished information on the fate or whereabouts of the missing, and the number arrested and detained by each side during the independence struggle remains unknown.

On July 4, 1989, 153 detainees who had been held by SWAPO returned to Windhoek after their release from camps in southern Angola. Their testimony was highly damaging to SWAPO, and it became politically explosive. During the election campaign for the Constituent Assembly in September and October 1989, the parties opposed to SWAPO made the treatment of detainees a major issue. Ex-detainees displayed their physical scars at campaign rallies and described their treatment in the SWAPO camps. Mr. Theo-Ben Guirab, SWAPO's Foreign Secretary, publicly regretted the brutal treatment, adding that abusive interrogators would be held responsible for their actions (a promise the government has failed to honor); and that if the matter was not properly dealt with, the wounds of war could never heal.

Unfortunately, the humanitarian issues became a narrow partisan issue in the charged elections. The outcry prompted the Secretary General's Special Representative in Namibia to dispatch an investigative team, the United Nations Mission on Detainees (UNMD), to determine whether any Namibians were still held by SWAPO. The UNMD compiled lists with more than 1,100 names, but determined that there were no more detainees in SWAPO custody in either Angola or Zambia.

Following the election of a Constituent Assembly in November 1989 (in which SWAPO received a majority of the votes) and the drafting of a constitution, Namibia achieved independence on March 20, 1990. The new Namibian Constitution contains a detailed chapter of Fundamental Human Rights and Freedoms providing a framework for protection. Today Namibia is a multi-party democracy in which SWAPO governs. Its legislature, the National Assembly, is a forum for aggressive partisan debate. The country has an independent judiciary and a vigorous free press. In short, Namibia has made a difficult but real transition from the oppression of colonial rule to a functioning, if fragile, democracy.

Even so, past abuses continue to cast a shadow over this transition. Shortly after independence, the SWAPO-led government appointed officials from the South African colonial regime who had abused civilians to senior positions in Namibia's new security apparatus. SWAPO's policy of national reconciliation to heal the wounds of the independence struggle helped to forestall public opposition. Six months later, in October 1990, the government appointed Solomon Hawala as Commander of the Army. The head of SWAPO's security forces, Hawala (whose *nom de guerre* was "Jesus") had overseen the arrest, interrogation, torture and disappearance of SWAPO detainees in southern Angola. He was dubbed "the Butcher of Lubango." The Hawala appointment unleashed a storm of protest domestically and internationally. Organizations and individuals that had supported SWAPO during the independence struggle criticized it. SWAPO responded that its critics were calling for a "mass purge,

Nuremberg-type of trial and consequent retribution."[1] Abisai Shejavali, General Secretary of the Council of Churches in Namibia (CCN), replied in turn that:

> We are in no way calling for a 'Nuremberg type of trial.' Our point is that it is not wise to entrust the security of independent and democratic Namibia to persons who have allegedly violated human rights on a gross scale.[2]

Bitter debates such as this issue generated in Namibia have erupted in many countries. After studying these debates, Human Rights Watch adopted a policy on accountability for past abuses that is intended to set forth principles of general application. The full text of this policy appears in Appendix A. It provides that the most important means of establishing accountability is that the government should make known all the reliable information that can be published about such past gross abuses including: their nature and extent; the identities of the victims; the identities of those responsible for devising the policies; and the identities of those who carried out the policies. Human Rights Watch opposes amnesties for those responsible for gross abuses. While advocating criminal prosecution for those who have the highest responsibility for the most severe abuses, Human Rights Watch holds that accountability may be achieved by public disclosure in cases of lesser responsibility and/or less severe abuse.

In several countries where accountability has been a major issue, this has proven a difficult path to follow. There may be compelling reasons for a new government, attempting to move a nation beyond a legacy of abuse and divisive conflict, to overlook past abuses. Governments cite the need to heal the country's wounds and promote reconciliation. Indeed, in societies torn by violence, national reconciliation is an urgent task, yet experience suggests that such reconciliation requires a recognition and acknowledgment of great crimes and great suffering. Mere forgetfulness glosses over, but does not heal, the damage caused by gross violations of rights. As the victims of such abuses and their families have repeatedly emphasized, for reconciliation to be meaningful, it is essential that the past should not be denied.

Interviews with former SWAPO detainees conducted by Africa Watch, made it clear that many want to help to build an independent Namibia, but believe this must be based on a thorough accounting of what happened. According to one former detainee:

> It is necessary to clear this up. To say just forget the past, then reconciliation will remain superficial. If I am going to reconcile myself, I have to know what I am reconciling myself to. Otherwise a lot of people will remain with the same questions that they had three years ago or even nine years ago. Many of us don't have bitterness—we want to be part of the process but we can't unless we get answers to the questions that we have. We're caught in between—Koevoet, **SADF**

---

[1] "Pack and Go Critics of 'Jesus' Are Told," *The Namibian*, October 25, 1990

"CCN Hits Out at SWAPO Paper on 'Jesus' Issue," *The Namibian*, November 2, 1990.

did such terrible things, you can't forget that and you can't forget the details of 100 years of oppression in this country. It's a Catch 22 situation.

A newly elected government often has only a fragile command over the country's armed forces and may be reluctant to antagonize the military by pursuing accountability. Restive armed forces pose a grave danger to a new government. In such circumstances, officials often contend that insistence on accountability on behalf of a relative few could jeopardize the new democratic order that benefits the great majority. Yet even adherents of this utilitarian view should recognize that the failure to hold past abusers to account might encourage those responsible to believe they are above the law, and thereby enhance the prospect of future violations.

Identifying the victims of great abuses of rights and documenting their suffering is a means that a society has to acknowledge their individual worth and dignity. Naming the names of those responsible for that suffering is a way for society to condemn that conduct. In addition, disclosing and acknowledging the truth may help to prevent similar abuses from occurring again.

In Namibia today it is clear that the wounds caused by the abuses committed during the war have not healed. For the victims, their families and friends, it is not possible to simply forget. According to one former detainee held by the South Africans who was tortured by his jailers:

> To heal the wounds there must a fair process. How can there be reconciliation when so many disappeared. It is necessary to follow up against the South Africans with damages claims for property and crops destroyed. To heal, something has to be done in the form of compensation. But nothing has been done.

Similar views have been expressed by former detainees held by SWAPO. One detainee spoke to Africa Watch about the disappearances:

> It's an issue for the parents who are not SWAPO members but whose children were. These parents don't know where their children are. This issue will not go away of its own. The families are in pain. They hear from someone that their relative was seen in Luanda and they hear that their child is dead. This is why this has to be resolved.

Some former SWAPO detainees wonder whether their colleagues still remain in detention. One former detainee told Africa Watch:

> I don't believe they could have been killed because there were just too many. They [SWAPO] couldn't have killed all of them. Many must still be in Angola. I don't know in whose hands. We get many bits of information. Neither UNTAG nor Angola acted on these leads.

These victims do not accept that their suffering was simply an inevitable consequence of the war:

> In response to the argument that the South Africans did it too, we cannot equate South African colonial rule with SWAPO. The organization has always been seen as being different from the enemy. It's ridiculous to equate ourselves with the South Africans. We've never been the same. While the South Africans have tortured our people...SWAPO has tortured its own people.

> Many people will say that it was the war and that these things happen during a war. My view is that no amount of wrongs ever make a right. You can't use the war as an excuse to cover things over, to hide them under the carpet.

Africa Watch publishes this report and the recommendations in it, to press the governments concerned—South Africa and Namibia—to begin accounting for the abuses: that is, to release information that helps to establish the truth. We are aware that, in June 1991, the government of Namibia asked the International Committee of the Red Cross (ICRC) to investigate the cases of those who went missing during the struggle. Over the last year the ICRC has done its utmost to follow through on the tracing requests submitted to it. In April 1992, the organization held a press conference in Windhoek calling for the submission of new requests. As of the middle of June it had received more than 1700 requests from family members for missing relatives. This indicates the scope of the problem. Yet as an humanitarian organization, the ICRC's tracing work is limited to:

> obtaining, registering, collating and when necessary forwarding information about people helped by the ICRC; re-establishing contact between separated family members; tracing persons reported missing or whose relatives are without news; drawing up death certificates.[3]

The ICRC does not make determinations about culpability. What is required is, as in other countries, the establishment of a Truth Commission that would establish what happened or in the words of one former detainee lead to "a frank and open discussion of what happened." Anything less evades the responsibility that the governments of South Africa and Namibia must assume.

Africa Watch also has a broader purpose in publishing this report. We hope that its publication will contribute to the establishment of an historical record. By setting forth the testimony and experiences of the victims of both the South African regime and SWAPO, we signify our respect for them and for their suffering. By calling attention to their experiences, we hope that this report enhances awareness of what happened. Yet this is no substitute for what

---

[3] International Committee of the Red Cross, *Annual Report*, 1989, p. 8.

governments must do; it is only the governments that can acknowledge responsibility and, thereby, begin the process of reparations.

Africa Watch is aware that the treatment of the former SWAPO detainees remains a highly charged political question in Namibia. It was a volatile issue during the hard fought election campaign for the Constituent Assembly.[4] The parties opposing SWAPO used the treatment of the detainees as a political cudgel. According to one former SWAPO detainee:

> During the election campaign this issue was unfortunately used by certain organizations—that's the nature of an election campaign. It was a sensational issue—it drew a lot of sympathy.

Since independence, the issue of the SWAPO detainees has periodically been the focus of sharp controversy and debate in the National Assembly and the opposition press.

Africa Watch understands that the publication of this report may be seized upon to further the partisan political agenda of groups and individuals who have no concern for human rights in Namibia. We hope that with the election well past, the truth-telling process that needs to take place can occur with a minimum of partisan political posturing. In any event, Africa Watch believes that an accounting of the abuses by both sides should not be withheld because some may try to exploit this for partisan advantage.

---

[4] Subsequent disclosures revealed that the South African government poured $35 million into the campaign in an effort to support the party of its choice, the Democratic Turnhalle Alliance (DTA). Christopher Wren, "Pretoria Spent $35 Million To Influence Namibian Vote," *New York Times*, July 26, 1991. p. 3.

2. GERMAN AND SOUTH AFRICAN COLONIAL RULE

GERMAN COLONIAL CONQUEST

In 1883–4, Adolf Luderitz, a German businessman, gained control over an area around Angra Pequena, a bay on South West Africa's southern coast. He had made a cunning trading agreement with Nama Chief Joseph Fredericks of Bethanie that gave Luderitz the rights to the area. This agreement provided a foothold for German economic and political interests and was soon followed by the establishment of German colonial rule. Luderitz named a settlement he founded there after himself. At the Conference of Berlin in 1885, where the European powers divided Africa into spheres of domination, South West Africa became a German protectorate. To consolidate its rule, the Germans exploited competition over land and cattle to divide the Territory's indigenous ethnic groups. The colonists also resorted to force to obtain "protection treaties" that effectively gave them use of tribal lands.

As early as 1896, two chiefs of the eastern Herero ethnic group rose up in protest against German encroachment on their land. Another Herero chief, Samuel Maherero, supported by the Germans, sided with the colonial regime to suppress the rebellion. The two chiefs were executed and the cattle belonging to their people was confiscated.

Eight years later, angered by the brutal treatment of the Herero people, Samuel Maherero, launched a rebellion against the Germans. In a letter to the German governor, Maherero wrote:

> The war wasn't started just this year by me, but was started by the white people; for you know how many Hereros have been killed by white people . . . with rifles and in prisons. And always when I brought these cases to Windhoek the blood of the people was valued at no more than a few head of small stock.[1]

An order was circulated among the Herero that no women, children, unarmed or non-German Europeans were to be attacked. Under-Chief Daniel Karikp, stated in a subsequent affidavit:

> We decided that we should wage war in a humane manner and would kill only German men who were soldiers . . . and then not young boys who could not fight . . . . We met at secret councils and there our chiefs decided that we should spare the lives of all German women and children. The missionaries too were to be spared, and they, their wives and families and possessions were to be protected by our people from all harm.[2]

---

[1] John Swan, "The Final Solution in South West Africa," *Military History Quarterly*, June 1991, p. 45.

[2] Peter Katjavivi, *A History of Resistance in Namibia*, (Paris: UNESCO Press, 1987), p. 8.

Efforts to coordinate the Herero uprising with a rebellion by the Namas in the south failed. Because some German troops were deployed in the south for a time, the Hereros temporarily seized the military initiative. More than 100 German men—settlers and soldiers—were killed. Railroad lines and telegraph wires were destroyed along with a number of settler farms, but the families were spared. After six months of fighting, the Germans summoned reinforcements and appointed Lieutenant General Lothar Von Trotha as their new military commander. Von Trotha had earlier succeeded in putting down resistance to German colonial rule in East Africa. Under his command a decisive battle took place at Hamakari, east of Otjozondjupa (Waterberg). He assembled 4,000 troops, thirty-six artillery pieces and fourteen machine guns.[3] German troops surrounded an encampment of 50,000 Herero men, women and children densely packed into an area five miles wide and ten miles long and killed thousands of non-combatants. The Herero commanders, realizing the battle was lost, fled to the southeast, a weak point in the German lines, across the Omaheke Desert. This was part of the German military plan. According to a German General Staff paper, "The arid Omaheke was to complete what the German army had begun: the extermination of the Herero nation." One man who served with the colonial military as a guide later testified:

> I was present at Hamakari, near Waterberg, when the Hereros were defeated in a battle. After the battle, all men, women and children, wounded and unwounded, who fell into the hands of the Germans were killed without mercy. The Germans then pursued the others, and all stragglers on the roadside and in the veld were shot down and bayonetted. The great majority of the Herero men were unarmed and could make no fight. They were merely trying to get away with their cattle.[4]

Hendrik Campbell, who commanded a unit of native troops described an incident after the battle:

> When the fight was over we discovered eight or nine Herero women who had been left behind. Some of them were blind. They had food and water. The German soldiers burned them alive in the huts in which they lay.[5]

The Germans poisoned the water holes along the Omaheke's rim. The colonial troops later found holes that the Hereros had dug by hand in a search for water.[6] Captured Hereros were enslaved to build railroads.

---

[3] Jon M. Bridgman, *The Revolt of the Hereros*, (Berkeley: University of California Press, 1981), p. 121.

[4] Ibid., p. 50.

[5] Ibid., p. 126; quoting Drechsler, *Sudewestafrika,* p. 186.

[6] Ibid., p. 127.

In October 1904, General Von Trotha issued an order authorizing the extermination of the Hereros:

> inside German territory every Herero tribesman, armed or unarmed, with or without cattle, will be shot. No women and children will be allowed in the territory: they will be driven back to their people or fired upon . . . . I believe that the Herero must be destroyed as a nation.[7]

At the same time, the Nama peoples, led by Chief Hendrik Witbooi, rebelled against the Germans and the focus of battle shifted south. Witbooi was killed in combat in 1905, but the struggle was continued by guerrilla bands until 1907–8. One band, under Jakob Morenga, delivered a serious blow to the Germans in a battle in the Great Karas Mountains, near the Orange River. As a result of joint German-British operations, Morenga was slain and other guerrilla leaders were killed or bought off.

The number of indigenous people killed in these campaigns was staggering. By the end of 1905, some 75–80 percent of the Hereros had perished; the total Herero population was reduced from 60–80,000 to 16,000. Many died in German concentration camps.[8] By 1911, 35 to 50 percent of the remaining Namas had been killed, leaving a population of some 9,000.[9] Those taken prisoner were treated harshly, and many were deported to other German colonial holdings in Africa.

The surviving Hereros and Namas were governed harshly. According to one observer, "Their status was that of forced laborers, differing from that of slaves only in that they were not the property of their masters and so could not be bought or sold." The wars had a profound effect on the indigenous communities of the center and south: "It was a catastrophe, caused not only by the effects of the war but by German measures during the war and the native policies of the post-war years."[10] The Germans had confiscated their lands and cattle. All Africans were required to wear identification tags. Land was expropriated and given to arriving German settlers. Cattle raising and traditional forms of social organization were prohibited in an effort to render the population docile subjects of colonial rule. In 1911, Germany created a "Police Zone," comprising the lower three-quarters of South West Africa which was to be directly administered by imperial officials. Africans in the area were forbidden by law to own land, and by 1911, most of the valuable land in the center and south previously owned by Africans was controlled by settlers. The dispossessed peoples from the center and south were compelled by

---

[7] Katajvivi, *Resistance*, p. 10; citing H. Bley *South West Africa Under German Rule* (London: Heinemann, 1971), p. 149.

[8] Ibid.

[9] Ibid.

[10] Ibid.

a series of pass and vagrancy laws to work as wage laborers. Any African without visible means of support was punished as a vagrant. German employers enjoyed extensive powers of arrest[11] and Africans sentenced to prison terms were assigned to private and public employers alike. At the copper and diamond mines, conditions were abysmal, resulting in high mortality rates.

With the expansion of copper and diamond mining, the need for contract laborers increased. Though the Germans neither controlled nor administered the north (the area beyond the "Police Zone") the Ovambo people of the north became a major source of contract labor; by 1911, 10,000 Ovambo contract laborers worked in the mines and on the railways.[12]

SOUTH AFRICAN COLONIAL RULE

During World War I, South African troops invaded South West Africa at the request of the British. The South African forces quickly defeated the German units stationed in the Territory, and Windhoek was seized on May 12, 1915.[13] The South Africans appointed a military governor who declared martial law throughout the Territory. Eager to subdue the north and establish the Territory's boundary, the South Africans united with the Portuguese troops in Angola. In 1917, a joint South African-Portuguese expedition defeated the Ovambos and killed the leading chief, Mandume. His severed head was brought to Windhoek for display. South Africa's Administrator reported:

> The country is now entirely tranquil. Our representatives in Ovamboland will continue to watch the situation closely and do all in their power to induce able-bodied men of the different tribes to go south to engage themselves as laborers on the railways, mines and farms . . . . The supply from the Ukuanyama tribe has been much interrupted of late owing to Mandume's actions, but I am hopeful that it will soon be restored.[14]

At the Versailles Peace Conference, Germany was stripped of its colonial possessions. South Africa's delegates proposed to annex South West Africa and based their claims on: 1) close economic and political ties; 2) South Africa's security interests; and 3) the fact that South Africa had effectively governed the Territory for four years during the war. Though these arguments were supported by British Prime Minister Lloyd George and the French Minister for

---

[11] Ruth First and Ronald Segal ed., *South West Africa: A Travesty of Trust*, (London: Andre Deutsche, 1967), Robert L. Bradford, "Blacks to the Wall," p. 89.

[12] Katjavivi, *Resistance*, p. 11.

[13] First and Segal ed., *Travesty of Trust*, Wm. Roger Louis, "The Origins of the Scared Trust," p. 39.

[14] Ruth First, *South West Africa*, (Baltimore: Penguin, 1963), p. 99.

Colonies, an opposing proposal advocated by U.S. President Woodrow Wilson prevailed, a mandate system that he declared preferable ethically and more likely to ensure peace. Wilson believed that the wishes of the inhabitants should be ascertained and that it was "up to the Union of South Africa to make it so attractive that South West Africa would come to the Union of its own free will."[15]

On December 17, 1920, the newly constituted League of Nations entrusted South West Africa to the Union of South Africa as a "Class C" mandated territory,[16] meaning that the country was to be administered under the laws of the mandatory power as an integral part of its territory.

The Mandate went into effect on January 1, 1921, when martial law declared by South Africa ended in the Territory.

The end of German colonial rule had aroused expectations among the surviving Herero and Nama peoples that the land confiscated by the Kaiser's imperial administration would be returned to them. At the time, South Africa portrayed itself as the champion of Namibia's people. When the South Africans took control of Namibia, they compiled a detailed account of the conditions under German imperial rule. Known as the *Blue Book on Namibia*, it condemned the Germans for cruelty and indifference to the needs of the indigenous people.

Despite some initial changes, however, South African rule proved similar to German colonialism. The South African Administrator General quickly decreed that the land confiscated by Germans from the Hereros and Namas would not be returned; rights to that land had vested despite the Germans' ill-treatment of their colonial subjects.[17] One South African official acknowledged that little changed under the Mandate for the Territory's blacks:

> They [the Africans] soon realised that conditions would remain practically the same . . . as they were in German times.[18]

The South African regime said that the Hereros should be allocated desolate land tracts close to the Botswana border, the region where thousands had been massacred following General von Trotha's extermination order in 1904.

---

[15] R. W. Imshue, *South West Africa: An International Problem*, (London: Pall Mall Press, 1965), p. 5.

[16] Mandates were divided into categories representing descending capacities for self-government.

[17] David Soggot, *Namibia: The Violent Heritage*, (London: Rex Collings, 1986), p. 17.

[18] First and Segal, eds, *A Travesty of Trust*, Robert L. Bradford, "Blacks to the Wall," p. 90.

GOVERNANCE, LAND AND GRAND APARTHEID

From the outset, the South Africans dispossessed and disenfranchised the indigenous population. The Territory was governed by an Administrator General appointed by the South African government; only whites were permitted self-government. The 1925 South West Africa Constitution Act established a Legislative Assembly of twenty-four members, six were appointed and eighteen were elected. Voting was governed by the electoral laws of South Africa, which denied African suffrage. Membership in the Assembly was limited to those eligible to vote. The Assembly had limited powers; South Africa's Parliament retained control over Native Affairs, Defence and Justice. There was an Advisory Council to the Administrator with one member appointed "by reason of his thorough acquaintance with the reasonable wants and wishes of the non-European races of the Territory."[19]

The new colonial regime actively encouraged South African settlers to immigrate, providing financial incentives, and their number increased dramatically. During the first year of the Mandate, land was allocated to 200 white settler families. The following year, the white population doubled despite the repatriation of 6,000 German settlers.[20] Between 1920 and 1926, 1,200 settlers arrived. They were allocated large grants of land.[21]

At the same time the South African administration established segregated areas for Africans. The Native Administration Proclamation Act of 1922 authorized "Native Reserves" and regulations for their control and administration. The same year, a Native Reserves Commission proposed that 10 percent of the land in the central and southern parts of the country should be set aside for the indigenous population. In all, approximately 8.8 million hectares were allocated for tribal reserves; of these, 8 million were dry *sandveld*. Africans were increasingly forced into designated sandveld areas that were not suitable for livestock grazing. The "Native Reserve" for the Namas allocated 990 hectares per family. Given the poor quality of the designated land, this was grossly inadequate to sustain life.[22] A pattern of forced removals continued until the 1960s.

---

[19] First and Segal, eds., *Travesty of Trust*, Kozonguizi and O'Dowd, "The Legal Apparatus of Apartheid," p. 120.

[20] Soggot, *The Violent Heritage*, p. 20.

[21] First, *South West Africa*, p. 107.

[22] Robert Rothberg ed., *Namibia: Political and Economic Prospects*, (Lexington Mass: Lexington Books, 1983), Nicholas H.Z. Watts, "The Roots of Controversy," p. 4.

The Native Administration Proclamation Act of 1928 authorized the Administrator to move ethnic groups from one area to another.[23] A quarter of a century later, however, the South West Africa Native Affairs Administration Act of 1954 transferred responsibility for "native affairs" to the South African Minister of Bantu Administration and Development. Control over Africans in the Territory was thus incorporated directly into the administration of South Africa. By several subsequent proclamations, additional powers were delegated to the South African Minister of Bantu Administration and Development until full authority over Africans was vested in Pretoria.

Over the years the forced removal of Africans to designated reserves created a vast pool of laborers to work in the white areas. To enhance control over Africans, a series of laws was passed to regulate movement of all blacks.[24] The Vagrancy Proclamation No. 25 of 1920 made the jobless subject to imprisonment under the criminal law. Courts could compel defendants to work at a predetermined wage for white farmers. Also, in 1920, the Masters and Servants Proclamation prohibited Africans from leaving white employment under most conditions.[25] The Native Administration Proclamation No. 11 of 1922 created a "Pass Law system." Blacks were required to carry identification documents; without such papers, they were subject to criminal prosecution. To move about the country, special permits were required. Under Proclamation No. 33 of 1922, a curfew was imposed on blacks. Without written authorization by an employer, they were prohibited to be on the streets at night.[26] These laws controlling movement, residence and labor blatantly violated the terms of the Mandate granted by the League of Nations.

Those most severely exploited were the contract workers from the north. Men were compelled to accept labor under a contract of twelve to eighteen months duration. They had no choice and were assigned to one of three different types of work. Wages were fixed and those who quit faced criminal penalties. At the contract's expiration, the worker was obligated to return to his area, whether he desired to or not,[27] a system the International Commission of Jurists called "akin to slavery." Not surprisingly, the contract system gave rise to numerous strikes and labor actions.

In 1958-59, a campaign of forced removals was announced to remove blacks from an area of Windhoek known as Old Location. It was a shanty town district where Namibian families

---

[23] First and Segal, eds., *Travesty of Trust*, Kozonguizi and O'Dowd, "The Legal Apparatus of Apartheid," p. 119.

[24] Soggot, *The Violent Heritage*, p. 18.

[25] First and Segal, eds., *Travesty of Trust*, Kozonguizi and O'Dowd, "The Legal Apparatus of Apartheid," p. 125.

[26] Soggot, *The Violent Heritage*, p. 18.

[27] First and Segal, eds., *A Travesty of Trust*, Charles Kuraisa, "The Labor Force," p. 192.

had lived for generations; families had freehold rights to the land; and there was a strong community spirit. The South Africans claimed that better facilities would be available in Katutura, a new township five miles outside Windhoek. At the same time, the mixed race population would be relocated to a separate township, Khomasdal, that offered better housing and facilities than Katutura.[28] Several people were killed when a protest rally was forcibly dispersed by the administration.

In the 1960s, South Africa moved to establish a regime of Bantustans (artificial "homelands" created for African ethnic groups in South Africa) in the Territory. The Odendaal Commission, appointed to define the terms of apartheid in South West Africa, issued its report in 1964 calling for ten "homelands." Implementation would require the relocation of 28 percent of the African population. The remainder of the Territory, 60 percent of Namibia's land area, was reserved for the white population—some 100,000 people.[29] The Odendaal Plan was a blueprint for a "grand apartheid" scheme characterized by the complete separation of blacks from whites, the separation of Africans along ethnic lines and the dispersal of the African population to rural reserves incapable of supporting the projected population. According to one estimate, 80–90 percent of the Damaras, Namas and Hereros would be affected.[30] The stated objective was to create ethnically separate areas that would progress through "self-government" to eventual "independence." Citizenship rights would be accorded to the people of each homeland, precluding a right to a common national citizenship. Africans would become guest workers in the areas reserved for whites.

In 1967, the first homeland was created in Ovamboland. Though the homeland administration exercised limited control over education, justice, finance and community affairs, important decisions had to be approved by Pretoria. Similar administrations were established in Okavangoland and East Caprivi in 1970 and 1972. In 1971, the establishment of a homeland for Damaras—Damaraland—was proposed. This was blocked by prospective members of an advisory council, however, and never implemented. The ethnic homeland of Kaokoland was created in 1975. The Hereros managed to block plans for a Herero homeland.

Despite increasing pressure at the United Nations, South Africa refused to transfer its mandate to the United Nations Trusteeship system. Pretoria was still intent on making Namibia its *de facto* and, ultimately, *de jure,* fifth province. It justified its refusal by claiming that the overwhelming majority of the Territory's inhabitants desired incorporation into South Africa.

---

[28] Nicholas H.Z. Watts, "The Roots of Controversy," p. 1

[29] Soggott, *The Violent Heritage*, p. 34.

[30] Ibid.

In 1960, Ethiopia and Liberia, two states that had been members of the defunct League of Nations, brought suit against South Africa before the International Court of Justice (ICJ) for violating Mandate obligations. In 1966, however, the Court refused to issue a ruling on the merits because it found that Ethiopia and Liberia lacked standing to bring an action over the administration of the Territory. The case was dismissed. This ICJ decision helped to prompt SWAPO to initiate an armed struggle for the independence of Namibia and the first military encounter occurred in August 1966.

3. BACKGROUND TO THE WAR

SOUTH AFRICAN FORCES

SADF and SWATF

Pretoria deployed an array of military, para-military, security and police forces to wage its counter-insurgency campaign. By 1986, it was estimated that there were some 60,000 SADF troops, most of them conscripts, in Namibia. SADF first began organizing units of black Namibians in 1974 and established additional "homeland" units in 1976 and 1977.[1] In the late 1970s and early 1980s, the South Africans systematically began to re-organize their forces in order to more thoroughly "Namibianize" the conflict. The SADF sought to recruit black Namibians into the armed forces to sow divisions among the population; to reduce casualty rates among white South Africans; to transform the independence struggle into a civil war; and to alleviate manpower shortages.[2] In April 1980, the Administrator General of Namibia announced that a transfer of "some control" over military and police forces would begin once the necessary structures were in place.

While the newly established Council of Ministers[3] had the authority to draft soldiers, Pretoria retained functional command over the military units in Namibia. In August 1980, the South West Africa Territorial Force (SWATF) was launched, recruited and organized along ethnic lines. By mid-1985, the strength of SWATF was reported officially to be 21,000 with just over 60 percent said to be black.[4] At a press briefing in June 1985, General George Mering, Commander of SADF and SWATF, said that up to 40,000 South African and Namibian soldiers were on the Angolan border, 61 percent of them Namibians.

Koevoet

The effort to organize para-military forces was accelerated in the late 1970s. The most infamous unit was *Koevoet*—"Crowbar" in Afrikaans—otherwise known as the Special Operations K Unit of the South African Security Police. This special counter-insurgency unit was modelled after the Selous Scouts of Rhodesia, a unit of black Rhodesians who had been known to disguise themselves as insurgents during the war there.[5] Hans Dreyer, a Colonel in the South

---

[1] Gavin Cawthra, *Brutal Force: The Apartheid War Machine*, (London: International Defence and Aid Fund for Southern Africa, 1986), p. 199.

[2] Ibid.

[3] In 1980, the Administrator General's Advisory Council was converted into a Council of Ministers that consisted of twelve members. Each member represented a pulation group. The Administrator General was empowered to veto decisions of the Council and act independently in times of emergency.

[4] Ibid.

[5] Cawthra, *Brutal Force*, p. 123.

African Security Police in Natal Province, was appointed to form the unit in late 1978.[6] Though Koevoet functioned as a para-military force, it was designated a police unit. The "police" designation had a particular significance: under the terms of UN Resolution 435, police units would continue to carry out their functions during the transition to elections and independence. Thus, Koevoet, as a police unit, would be charged with maintaining order during the elections.

Koevoet numbered no more than 3,000, including a core of white officers recruited from the ranks of the South African Police, the Selous Scouts, and other former Rhodesian mercenaries.[7] Ninety percent of Koevoet's personnel was black, recruited predominantly from the Ovambo population. Koevoet constables were not recruited through the usual police or security recruitment process. They were drawn from the poorly educated, and often had criminal records. Later Koevoet recruits came from the ranks of UNITA (União Nacional para a Independência Total de Angola) and the FNLA (Frente Nacional de Libertação de Angola) in Angola. Captured SWAPO guerrillas were also coerced into joining. Among many in the north Koevoet personnel were known as *makakunya* (bloodsuckers).

For a time, Koevoet's existence was kept secret. Its existence became public in June 1980 when a local religious newspaper printed an article about a South African force specially created to assassinate prominent individuals in Ovamboland believed to be sympathetic to SWAPO. The article named fifty people who were alleged to be on a "death list"; several of those on the list had already died in mysterious or suspicious circumstances. Reportedly, these individuals were to be eliminated before the election that would determine the country's future.[8] Though denying the existence of the death list, the South African authorities acknowledged the unit's existence and praised its effectiveness.

In court cases filed against Koevoet, it was revealed that the unit had access to uniforms and weapons similar to those used by SWAPO combatants. Koevoet members received a bounty payment (*kopgeld*) for every alleged PLAN combatant they killed. Koevoet reportedly achieved a "kill ratio" of PLAN combatants twenty-five times greater than that of the SADF.[9] During its ten years' existence, Koevoet reportedly had 1,615 military engagements with PLAN units. It killed 2,812 PLAN fighters and captured 463 against a loss of 151 killed in action.[10] In addition

---

[6] Peter Stiff, *Nine Days of War and South Africa's Final Days In Namibia*, (Johannesburg: Lemur Books, 1991), p. 142.

[7] Cawthra, *Brutal Force*, p. 124.

[8] Jonathan Steele, "Fifty named in death list," *The Guardian* [U.K.], June 9, 1980.

[9] D. Herbstein and J. Evenson, *The Devils Are Among Us; The War For Namibia*, (London: Zed, 1989), p. 64.

[10] Stiff, *Nine Days of War*, p. 142.

to launching "track and destroy" missions against PLAN fighters infiltrating or operating in Ovamboland or Okavango, Koevoet terrorized the civilian population of the north.

Prior to 1985, Koevoet came under the jurisdiction of the South African Security Police. In 1985, Koevoet's name was officially changed to the South West Africa Police Counter Insurgency Unit (SWAPOL COIN) and the unit was ostensibly transferred to SWAPOL's control. Koevoet remained under the control of the SADF. While the command structures had been separate, SWAPOL's Security Police and Koevoet had always worked closely together, often exchanging detainees for interrogation purposes. South Africa's Minister of Law and Order acknowledged Koevoet's origins and aims in a Parliamentary debate:

> Furthermore we have the Koevoet unit which started out with a small number of Security Police officers. This unit was formed at the request of the Defence Force and their duty is to act as the eyes and ears of and to collect information for the military. The Koevoet grew eventually to its present strength of approximately 1,000 men. Approximately 750–800 of these men are from the local population who are basically trained for two or three months and then posted to the Koevoet unit, while some of them are posted to the *kraals* [traditional Ovambo homesteads] of headmen to do security duties. They are under the command of a SA Police officer, and in all there are about 200 South African policemen involved in Koevoet. The rest of the Koevoet unit are members of the South West African Police. They are paid on our account. But the unit as such is the responsibility of the Minister of Law and Order in South Africa. This unit basically started off as our eyes and ears but they have developed into a strong military machine.[11]

Security Police

The South African Security Police, a separate branch of the police structure, had a large contingent assigned to Namibia. With units at many police bases, the Security Police were responsible for the interrogation of political prisoners and witnesses.[12]

Prior to 1980, the police in Namibia were part of the South African Police (SAP). The Commissioner of the South African Police commanded the police forces in Namibia and all police powers in South Africa applied there. In September 1980, ministerial control of the police in Namibia was transferred from the South African Minister of Police to the Administrator

---

[11] Manfred Hinz and Nadia Gevers Leuven-Lachinski, *Koevoet Versus The People of Namibia,"* *Report of A Human Rights Mission to Namibia On Behalf of the Working Group Kairos*, (Utrecht: Netherlands, 1989), p. 5

[12] Cawthra, *Brutal Force*, p. 194.

General of the Territory. On April 1, 1981, the South African Police formally relinquished responsibility for policing Namibia to the newly created South West African Police (SWAPOL). South African police officers in Namibia were given the choice of joining SWAPOL or remaining on "secondment" there.[13] However, this transfer of command did not include the Security Police. The Security Police remained directly under the control of the SAP until May 1985, when it became part of SWAPOL.[14] The impact of these changes was cosmetic and had little effect on the conduct of the war; SWATF and SWAPOL functioned as administrative subsections of the SADF and SAP.[15]

Homeguards

The South Africans also established units known as Homeguards. Their principal function was to protect homeland leaders, but they were also used to patrol, and they received some counter-insurgency training. Heavily armed, these units supported SADF patrols,[16] particularly in Ovamboland.[17] Later these forces came under the command of SWAPOL. Their conduct was commented on by the *Windhoek Observer* of February 6, 1982:

> Has the Home Guard system been created in order to build a counter-insurgency arm? . . . Or has it been created with the explicit objective to sow terror and murder people, and thereby to institute civil strife and war? With rare exceptions one can call the Home Guards gangsters. . . . They convey the impression . . . of vagrant drunkards, armed and wandering aimlessly around to shoot at random and to kill. They can be termed official exterminators . . ."[18]

SWAPO MILITARY FORCES

In 1973 SWAPO's military forces were named the People's Liberation Army of Namibia (PLAN). After Angola achieved independence, SWAPO moved its headquarters from Zambia to Luanda. PLAN established military bases in southern Angola and was based in Lubango. PLAN also maintained bases in Zambia from which it launched attacks across the Caprivi Strip in northeastern Namibia. In both these areas SWAPO provided military training to those Namibians

---

[13] *Focus*, May/June 1982.

[14] Amnesty International, "Namibia: The Human Rights Situation at Independence," AI Index: AFR 42/04/90, p. 5.

[15] "Restructuring of Police Force," *IDAF Focus* No. 26, January/February 1980, p. 9.

[16] Cawthra, *Brutal Force*, p. 194.

[17] Ibid., p. 199.

[18] Ibid., p. 200.

who had fled the country and joined the organization. In 1978, the South Africans claimed there were some 16,000 PLAN fighters; by 1985, they alleged this number had been reduced to 8,000.[19]

THE COURSE OF THE WAR

The war was fought in the north of the country and typically involved guerrilla engagements: hit and run attacks by PLAN and counter-insurgency sweeps against the guerrillas. The northern war zone, the "Operational Area," was divided into three zones by the South African command. Section 10, covering Ovamboland and Kaokoland, was the scene of most military activity and had at least eighty permanent army and police bases. Section 10's headquarters were in Oshakati.

Most South African military activity consisted of intensive patrolling, by relatively small groups scouring the bush for signs of PLAN combatants and stopping in the *kraals* and *cuca* shops (general stores which also doubled as pubs). On making contact with PLAN combatants, the patrols would pursue them and, when necessary, radio for reinforcements. In case of contact with a large PLAN unit, mobile reaction forces would be dispatched in armored personnel carriers. PLAN actions included attacks on military bases, sabotage, planting land mines, bombings and assassination of homeland leaders.

The armed insurgency began on August 26, 1966, when SWAPO fighters engaged in a shootout with South African forces near a guerrilla training camp that had been established at Omgulumbashe.[20] By the early 1970s, SWAPO had established several guerrilla bases in Zambia along the border of the Caprivi Strip. From these, guerrillas mined roads patrolled by South African police. After the collapse of Portuguese rule in Angola in 1975, SWAPO was able to move PLAN armed units into southern Angola, where they mingled with the Ovambo people living north of the Namibian border. SWAPO was soon able to infiltrate large numbers of combatants into Namibia. In a skirmish in 1975, sixty-one PLAN guerrillas were killed along with three South Africans. By the spring of 1976, the military threat was sufficient for the South African colonial authorities to declare emergency rule in the country's northern tier—Ovamboland, Kavangoland and the Caprivi Strip.[21]

By late 1977, PLAN guerrillas were engaging in frequent clashes in Ovamboland; the South Africans claimed there were 100 clashes every month. In 1977, South African forces

---

[19] Colin Legum, ed., *Africa Contemporary Record: Annual Survey and Documents 1983–84*, (New York: Africana Publishing Company, 1985), A13.

[20] Evensen and Herbstein, *The Devils Are Amongst Us*, p. 16.

[21] Robert S. Jaster, *South Africa in Namibia: The Botha Strategy*, (New York: University Press of America, 1985), p. 20

cleared a strip along 450 kilometers of the Angolan border to construct a security fence designed to halt infiltration from Angola. Nevertheless, SWAPO continued its hit and run tactics, including the assassination of homeland leaders.[22]

Security Legislation

The South African regime implemented a battery of security laws that established a regime of sweeping emergency powers giving the security forces unchecked latitude and facilitating gross abuses against civilians. Under the Security Districts Proclamation,[23] the authorities were empowered to declare "security districts": special orders could prohibit persons from entering or leaving such a district. The authorities could require persons to move from certain places, prohibit them from carrying on certain activities and from being outside designated places at night.[24] This Proclamation also authorized indefinite detention without charge or trial. A subsequent amendment allowed the authorities to prevent movement within a security district.[25] The districts of Ovambo, Kavango and Eastern Caprivi were all declared security districts.

Another government notice ordered that no one was to drive or travel in Ovamboland without an official permit "at any time during the night."[26] A subsequent decree stated that "no person shall be at any place in the district of Ovambo outside the boundary of a stand, lot or site or other place intended not normally used for human habitation, at any time during the night."[27]

The curfew disrupted life in Ovamboland, and put the entire civilian population at risk. On September 5, 1986, a legal challenge was filed to invalidate the curfew by the Bishop of the Anglican Diocese of Namibia, the Bishop of the Roman Catholic Church, Diocese of Windhoek, and the Bishop of the Evangelical Lutheran Church in Namibia. The case was dismissed.

South African legislation indemnified officials for acts committed in the fight against terrorism. AG 9 of 1977 barred civil actions "of any nature . . . against the State, any government or administration, the Administrator General . . . any member of the security forces or any person in the service of the State . . ."

---

[22] Ibid.

[23] Proclamation AG 9 of 1977.

[24] Ibid., Section 3(1)(a)(i), (ii), (iii), (iv) and (v).

[25] Proclamation AG 43 of 1978.

[26] Government Notice AG 26 of 1978.

[27] Government Notice AG 50 of 1978.

Another provision barred criminal prosecution of any security official for anything done in "good faith in the exercise of his powers or the performance of his duties" under the powers of the Proclamation.[28] During the 1980s, South African State President P.W. Botha intervened to halt prosecutions against security personnel charged with serious crimes. In addition to AG 9, Section 103 of the Defence Act granted immunity from prosecution to members of the security forces for acts carried out in "good faith" under operational conditions.[29]

The 1980s

While South Africa built up its forces and conducted an aggressive counter-insurgency campaign in the years immediately after 1978, SWAPO's numbers and capabilities, assisted by increasing supplies of Soviet arms and military instructors from Eastern Europe, continued to grow. By mid-1979, PLAN fighters were operating in the area of Grootfontein, a white farming district in the northeast. By 1981, a number of the farms in the Outjo District, another white farming area, had been abandoned.[30] Though PLAN's attacks were scattered, the organization had a tangible military presence in the north. In the area between Tsuemb, Otavi and Grootfontein at certain times road traffic would travel in convoy for protection. The deployment of PLAN units to the east of Etosha Pan occasionally disrupted transportation along the highway north of Oshivello.

During this period there was extensive infiltration across the Angolan border. Guerrilla attacks on police and army positions occurred frequently, along with mortar and rocket attacks on administrative centers.[31] SWAPO forces sabotaged power lines and blacked out a number of towns. In 1980, a mortar attack destroyed a number of aircraft at the South African base at Ondangwa. This period constituted the most intense phase of military combat.

In the summer of 1980, the South African military launched attacks across the border against SWAPO targets deep inside Angola. The attacks resulted in numerous casualties and logistical difficulties for SWAPO, which was forced to launch its attacks from ever greater distances. As a result, contacts dropped off and South African officials predicted a speedy demise to PLAN as a military force. Nevertheless, in April 1982, a detachment of some 100 guerrillas penetrated 130 miles south of the Angolan border to Tsuemb, site of a large copper mine. Using ever-more sophisticated weaponry, the guerillas killed nine South African soldiers and a smaller number of civilians. Nevertheless, the insurgency did not escalate qualitatively. SWAPO was unable to mount the kind of armed struggle that had taken place in Zimbabwe: the

---

[28] Section 8(2)(a).

[29] Cawthra, *Brutal Force*, p. 211.

[30] Soggot, *The Violent Heritage*, p. 286.

[31] Ibid.

strength of the South African forces, as well as Namibia's terrain, made that impossible. Though the SWAPO insurgency could not defeat the South Africans militarily in Namibia, neither could the South Africans eliminate PLAN without enormous cost to themselves.

PLAN activity continued during 1983. In July 1983 a powerful limpet bomb exploded in the center of Windhoek that caused extensive property damage but no injuries. This coincided with the promulgation of the State Council.[32]

In September 1983, 100 guerrillas entered the Ovambo and Kavango war zones activating the Security Force-Farmer Liaison Committee. That same month two landmines killed six and seriously injured ten passengers in a civilian vehicle near Rucana.[33]

In 1984–85, the war continued at a rate of nearly one incident a day, with a marked increase in sabotage bombings by PLAN forces. In July 1984, there was a reported increase in sabotage bombings by the guerrillas. Two Ovambo administration buses were damaged by a bomb in the center of Oshakati. Shortly after that a bomb exploded outside a store in Tsuemb. While no one was injured it was the twentieth such attack recorded in the region in a three month span. On July 31, two of a number of mortar bombs landed on the roof of Oshakati's hospital.[34]

The progress of the war became increasingly hard to track due to the difficulty of obtaining accurate information on troop strength and casualties. The two sides supplied widely varying of estimates of both. By 1984, SWATF reported PLAN casualties at a ratio of 21:1 (PLAN:SWATF). SWAPO countered by publishing statistics on South African forces killed in action that SADF denied. Both sides continued to dispute the other's claims of casualties. At a press conference in December 1984, for example, Major General George Meiring, head of the SADF and SWATF in Namibia, announced that there were no more than thirty active PLAN combatants in Namibia.[35] The counter-insurgency units of the army and police claimed that insurgents could only hope to survive for a week in Ovamboland before being tracked down and "eliminated." SWATF attributed this to the increasing flow of information from the local populace. According to senior officers, this indicated that the security forces were winning the battle for "hearts and minds."

---

[32] The State Council was proposed by South Africa's Administrator General. It was to be composed of fifty representatives from political parties and the private sector that would formulate a constitution which would be submitted for a referendum. It never took effect.

[33] Legum, ed., *African Contemporary Record: 1984–85*, B683.

[34] Barry Streak, "SWAPO 'losing' bush war in Namibia," *The Guardian*, December 21, 1984.

[35] Legum, ed., *African Contemporary Record: 1984–85*, B701.

There were a number of destructive bombings during 1985. The post office in Ondangwa was partially destroyed and several civilians were killed in New Year's 1985. A supermarket in Oshakati was also destroyed. Increased incidents of bombings and sabotage in which civilians were wounded and injured. [36]

For its part, in May 1986, SWAPO claimed it killed 164 soldiers in a series of devastating attacks; SADF reported the loss of seven members of the security forces that month.[37] In August 1986 a powerful bomb destroyed a butchery in Walvis Bay (the port on the Atlantic coast claimed as part of South Africa by Pretoria). Five people died and twenty were wounded. The South Africans blamed SWAPO which in turn denied involvement. At the same time, a bomb destroyed a gas station in Oshakati; the security forces later claimed that two SWAPO members were killed in the following operations.[38]

In April 1987, PLAN succeeded in infiltrating the farming areas around Etosha National Park for the first time since 1983. Throughout 1987, military communiques maintained that SWAPO was being forced to concentrate on sabotage operations and mortar and rocket attacks against military outposts or settlements because it was otherwise militarily ineffective.[39] Yet, the 1987 wet season infiltration by PLAN became one of the bloodiest campaigns in years for both sides. While SADF appeared to be taking a steady toll of PLAN fighters, PLAN appeared to be giving a better account of itself.

By the late 1980s, the war had reached a stalemate. The South Africans had succeeded in preventing serious cross border attacks and limited SWAPO to armed propaganda, while guerrilla activities were sufficient to tie down large numbers of South African troops.

At the end of the 1980s a series of increasingly bloody bombings took place for which neither side claimed responsibility. In February 1988, a massive bomb devastated the First National Bank branch in Oshakati, killing twenty-seven, the worst such explosion in southern Africa. Charges and counter charges were made back and forth. The authorities were quick to blame SWAPO, and revenge raids were launched the next day on SWAPO camps in southern Angola. However, broad sections of the population in the north did not believe that SWAPO was responsible as the majority of the dead and injured were black.

---

[36] Ibid.

[37] Legum, ed., *Africa Contemporary Record, 1985–86*, B705.

[38] Ibid., B706.

[39] Ibid., B709.

In the later years PLAN concentrated more on bombardments of settlements using small arms fire, rocket launchers mortars and recoilless rifles.[40] The war continued until Resolution 435 finally took effect in May 1989.

---

[40] Ibid.

4. BOMBING OF REFUGEE CAMPS AND DETENTIONS AT MARIENTAL

INTRODUCTION

South Africa's military and security forces waged a brutal twenty-three year counter-insurgency war to deny Namibia independence. In the course of the war they wantonly committed gross violations of international humanitarian law against the civilian population. The most egregious incident occurred when the SADF assaulted several refugee camps in southern Angola in May 1978. As a result of the attack, hundreds of civilians were killed and wounded. However, the record of abuse did not end with the military assault. Following the assault, the South Africans forcibly abducted at least two hundred Namibian refugees who had been living in the camps. They were transported across the international border between Angola and Namibia to SADF bases in northern Namibia. There they were interrogated and subjected to brutal torture for several weeks at camps around Oshakati. Over one hundred of the survivors were then transferred to a secret detention camp in southern Namibia near the town of Mariental. For several years the colonial authorities denied the Mariental camp even existed. One hundred eighteen Kassinga survivors were held there for six years. None was ever charged with a crime or given a trial.

ASSAULT ON THE CAMPS

On April 25, 1978, Prime Minister John Vorster told South Africa's Parliament in Capetown that his government accepted the proposals that had been issued by the Western members of the UN Security Council (the Contact Group) for a peaceful transition to Namibia's independence. The process would begin with several preliminary steps: the cessation of all hostile acts; the restriction of South African and PLAN forces to base; the phased withdrawal of the SADF troops; and the demobilization of citizen forces. These measures would be enforced, if necessary, by a military section of UNTAG. Political prisoners would be released and all refugees would be permitted to return to the country. The centerpiece of the proposals was the provision for the election of a Constituent Assembly which would draft a constitution. The election would be closely monitored by a the Special Representative of the Secretary General and a substantial force of UNTAG personnel.

Vorster's statement created optimism for an early end to the armed conflict. Nine days later, on May 4, 1978, the SADF attacked several Namibian refugee transit camps located in southern Angola. The largest of the camps, Kassinga, had buildings for classrooms and clinics. Located near the former Angolan mining town of the same name 250 kilometers (150 miles) north of the Namibian border, it covered a large area and housed some 3,000 refugees. An aerial attack on the camp was followed by a ground assault by 500 paratroopers of the 44th Paratroop Brigade, led by Colonel Jan Breytenbach.[1]

Camp dwellers who fled into the bush to escape bombardment were mowed down by gunfire. Most of the dead were shot at close range. The reported casualty figures were: 612

---

[1] Stiff, *Nine Days of War*, p. 140.

Namibian refugees killed; of these 147 were men, 167 were women and 298 were children. Twelve Angolan soldiers and three Angolan civilians were also reported killed. Six hundred and eleven Namibians, sixty-three Angolan soldiers and fifteen Angolan civilians were wounded.[2]

The South African authorities justified the attack by claiming that Kassinga was a military base. According to SADF accounts, by 1978 Kassinga had become SWAPO's main operational headquarters in southern Angola. These reports alleged that Kassinga was a training complex large enough to house between 700 and 1,200 insurgents. The SADF claimed that the camp contained various headquarters buildings, a large training complex, a parade ground, anti-aircraft gun emplacements and an extensive trench system. One account sympathetic to the South African military claimed that large stores of military supplies were found and destroyed there.[3]

On the other hand, SWAPO insisted that Kassinga was a refugee settlement, housing mostly women, children and old people. According to SWAPO, it contained a sewing factory and a garage. SWAPO stated that there were no military installations and only a small armed unit present to protect the camp. This contention was supported by independent film footage taken of Kassinga before the attack.[4] The camp appeared to be defended by a handful of guards.[5]

According to Luanda-based reporters who visited the camp after the raid, the corpses in the graves were mostly women and children[6] and most of the dead were dressed in civilian clothes.

Even if the camp had some military function, the SADF was bound by the laws of war to try to avoid civilian casualties. Under international humanitarian law the South Africans had a duty to distinguish and refrain from targeting civilians. This obligation was stated in a 1968 General Assembly Resolution which prohibited "attacks against the civilian population" and required a distinction be made at all times between "persons taking part in the hostilities and members of the civilian population" so that the civilians are spared as much as possible.[7] This obligation was further developed in Protocol I to the 1949 Geneva Conventions. Article 48 of Protocol I states that, "In order to ensure respect for and protection of the civilian population . . . the Parties to the conflict shall at all times distinguish between the civilian population and combatants . . ."

---

[2] Katjavivi, *Resistance*, p. 110.

[3] Willeim Steenkamp, *Borderstrike! South Africa into Angola*, (Durban: Butterworths, 1983) p. 19.

[4] "Behind the Carnage at Cassinga," *Africa*, No. 82., June 1978, p. 45.

[5] Soggot, *The Violent Heritage*, p. 231.

[6] Ibid.

[7] G.A. Res. 2444, 23 U.N. GAOR supp. (No. 18) at 164, U.N. Doc. A/&433 (1968).

Another of the camps attacked on May 4, 1978, was known as "Vietnam." This was located fifty kilometers from the Namibian border. Africa Watch interviewed Willie Amutenya, a former high school track star from the Ombaluntu district in northern Namibia. He was an active SWAPO member in Ombaluntu and fled the country in late 1977. On May 4, 1978, he was in the Vietnam camp. He had arrived there in mid-April. Today, Amutenya directs the Justice and Peace Commission of the Roman Catholic Church. He told Africa Watch:

On May 4, 1978, there were attacks on all three camps. Kassinga was attacked at 6:30 A.M., Vietnam was attacked at 1:00 P.M. Vietnam was fifty kilometers from the border. There were many civilians there waiting to be transferred.

Kassinga was a pure refugee camp; each camp was defended by a small contingent of soldiers so you can't say that there were no soldiers at the camp. This was a military zone in Angola: forces from the FNLA and UNITA were operating there. The SADF chose soft targets to break the bones of SWAPO.

Amutenya was injured by shrapnel. He crawled to a trench and lay there. He told Africa Watch that he saw soldiers shoot people lying in the trench he was in, some of whom were wounded, as well as those who tried to run away:

Vietnam was first attacked by planes and then later by ground forces. The attack lasted for 4–5 hours. Some people ran; some were injured like me and were lying in a trench. Many of the people who were lying in the trench were just shot. Others who started to run away were also shot. The evil of the whole thing was that they saw that people had no guns or even uniforms. I lost consciousness and later was picked up.

According to another man present at the Vietnam camp:

I, with some other comrades were on duty to prepare food that day, that is why we were still in the kitchen trying to wash the dishes when the first bombs fell and the first victim I saw was comrade Willie Amutenya whose right arm was converted into pieces of meat by the first bomb.[8]

After the attack was over, the SADF seized nearly 200 survivors at the camps and forcibly transported them across the Angolan border to military camps inside Namibia. These were refugees who had fled Namibia and had taken asylum in Angola. According to Willie Amutenya:

The SADF collected people and seized them at the Vietnam Camp. They loaded us on to lorries and we were taken to Otaapi [inside Namibia] where there was

---

[8] Speech by Pineas Aluteni given on the Tenth Anniversary of the Attack on the Kassinga Camp, reprinted by the Namibia Communications Centre, May 4, 1978, p. 5.

a big military camp. The next morning we were taken to Oshakati. On May 5, 1978, I was taken to Oshakati Hospital. It was the first time I saw Dr. Chris Barnard. He had come from Capetown to see the result of the military operation. There were big people from South Africa there—they were invited to see the South African success.

Amutenya's injured arm was amputated in Oshakati Hospital which was filled with other victims of the attack. Interrogations began in the medical wards:

From Oshakati Hospital I was brought to Ondangwa Sick Bay on May 6, 1978. That same day I was chained to the bed by my other wrist and I couldn't move. The hospital wards were full of Kassinga victims. They brought officials to question those of us in the hospitals.

The survivors of the camps who had been abducted across the border were severely tortured during interrogation by the South Africans. The authorities wanted information about SWAPO. One victim told Africa Watch that he was asked the names of those people who had helped him cross the border to Angola. Another man captured at the Vietnam camp was held for three months at a military base in Ovamboland. He told the Southern African Catholic Bishops Conference (SACBC) of horrific abuse:

Nearly all that time we were kept hanging from the wall, sometimes by our feet and sometimes by our hands. They used plastic sacks on our heads and electric shocks between our legs. Even if we told the truth we were tortured . . .[9]

One detainee told of being burned behind the ears and tortured with electricity.[10]

Achille Angulla, a survivor of the attack on the Vietnam camp, was among those transported back to Oshakati. In an interview with Africa Watch, he told of being beaten with freshly cut sticks and nearly suffocated with a bucket by the military police. This interrogation continued for nearly two weeks:

I was taken to a detention camp in Oshakati. The camp was divided into four units. By that time they had our names. We were called out one by one and told to go to tents. We were asked a number of questions: When did you join SWAPO? Why did you join SWAPO? Where did you get your information about SWAPO? Then questions about my family—how many brothers and sisters did I have?

I was subjected to electric shock and was beaten with fresh sticks. I was suspended by my wrists from a pole so that my feet didn't touch the ground. My

---

[9] "Detainees charged," *IDAF Focus* No. 58, June 1985, p. 4.

[10] Ibid.

head was covered with a bucket so that I couldn't breathe. We were punished in other ways as well—I was held for seven days without food for no reason at all. This was done by the military police. The interrogation process took nearly two weeks, day after day. People suffered physical weakness. For four years I couldn't sleep well. One of my friends had been asked to pick up rotten corpses and put them in the mortuary. He was told, "These are your fellow terrorists, pick them up."

Willie Amutenya, whose arm had just been amputated, was also interrogated. He told Africa Watch that many high ranking officials of the colonial government were present in Oshakati when the camp survivors were being tortured:

In the hospital they would push my bed into a separate room for interrogation. "Who helped you cross the border? How did you get food?" I told them, "if you give me back my arm I will tell you everything." That made them angry.

There were a lot of important South Africans around at that time: Dr. Chris Barnard; the Minister for the Ovambo homeland; the Administrator General for South Africa, Justice Steyn. Dirk Mudge of the DTA [Democratic Turnhalle Alliance] was there. The DTA was the ruling party at that time. We were told that the DTA asked for our detention without charge or trial because we were dangerous.

On May 29, 1978, the South Africans released sixty-three survivors in a public ceremony praising the "Christian spirit" of the soldiers who "rescued the young people from SWAPO." Shortly afterwards, Father Heinz Hunke, a Roman Catholic priest in Windhoek, was able to speak to those who had been released. A number of those he interviewed said they had been horribly tortured by white and black South African policemen during interrogation when their answers were not satisfactory. They described a general pattern of physical abuse endured by most of the detainees: beatings with fists and/or hard rubber sticks; kicking with boots in the kidneys, genitals and/or other parts of the body; extensive use of electric shock; and suspension from poles for up to four hours at a time. All of those interviewed by Father Hunke were firmly convinced that the remaining prisoners were being tortured.[11] South Africa's Administrator General rejected the allegations.[12]

According to Amutenya:

I was at the hospital for two and one half weeks. Sixty people had been released so we had hope of being released as well. Father Heinz Hunke wrote up the story

[11] Letter from Father Heinz Hunke to Administrator General Steyn, June 5, 1978.

[12] David Forrest, "SWA Torture Claims Untrue, Says Steyn," *Rand Daily Mail*, June 23, 1978.

of the torture that we were subjected to and the group that was released told the public what was happening for the first time.

After Amutenya was discharged from the hospital he was taken to a detention camp and interrogated for the names of those "cooperating with the terrorists:"

In the detention camp the police came in and asked me if I was Willie Amutenya. I said, "I know the person." They told me, "Here we can force you to speak." The police program was that you must give the name of one civilian who is cooperating with the "terrorists." That was the main purpose of the interrogation. Detainees from Kassinga were forced to tell the police who had helped them cross the border. Then that person would be arrested.

DETENTIONS AT MARIENTAL

After the interrogations were completed, 118 of the camp survivors who were not released were transported to a secret detention camp in southern Namibia. The camp was at Hardap Dam, twenty kilometers from Mariental. They were kept there for nearly six years. They were never charged with a crime by the South Africans. The Mariental detainees were held under the authority of Proclamation AG 9 of 1977 which empowered all members of the South African security forces of the rank of non-commissioned officer or above to detain people incommunicado without charge or trial for an initial thirty day period. Subsequently, the Administrator General was authorized to order unlimited detention. Families were not notified of arrest or place of detention, and security force personnel were indemnified for acts committed in "good faith." The South African authorities denied that the detainees were protected by the Geneva Conventions and labelled them common criminals. This designation was patently contradictory. On the one hand, if the detainees were combatants, as the SADF claimed in justifying the assault on the Kassinga camps, then they were entitled to the protections afforded prisoners of war by international humanitarian law. On the other hand, if they were not combatants, (a fact which would undercut the SADF's justification for the attack), they were entitled to protections granted civilians. Under no circumstances, could they legally be treated as ordinary criminals.

For the first few years the detainees were not allowed access to their families or to lawyers. For several years, the South African authorities even denied the existence of this camp. The commander of the SADF described reports about the detention camp as propaganda." In June 1980, two officials of the International Committee of the Red Cross (ICRC) were allowed to visit the camp. They reported that 118 people were being held there under the provisions of AG 9.[13] In 1981, the South Africans admitted that they were holding 117 SWAPO members captured at Kassinga. Namibian churches called for the release of the prisoners' names to end the

---

[13] International Defence and Aid Fund, "Remember Kassinga and Other Papers on Political Prisoners and Detainees in Namibia," (1981), p. 12.

uncertainty of the prisoners' family and friends.[14] In August 1982, a few detainees were visited by relatives for the first time.

The conditions at Mariental, especially in the early years, were miserable. There were no facilities at the camp and the prisoners were subjected to a strict regime which included hard labor. Food was poor and the detainees were not given sufficient clothing. They were not allowed to communicate with the outside world so that it was impossible to generate pressure for release or improvement in conditions. In an interview one Mariental detainee told Africa Watch:

> On August 17, 1978, we were told to collect our things and we were loaded on to lorries and brought to the airport at the Ondangwa Military base. We were flown down to the area of Mariental which is a semi-desert. There was barbed wire but that was all. We slept in tents and set up the camp. That was the toughest time. The guards at the camp were old soldiers from nearby farms. They had no mercy. Any movement and we would be shot. During the night you absolutely had to stay in your tent—you couldn't leave your block for another block except for those working in the kitchens. Thirty-five women were held in a separate block. The Camp Commander was named Leicher, a German speaking Catholic Namibian.

> It would get very cold and windy. We didn't have enough clothes. Food was very scarce. Nobody knew where we were, so they could do what they wanted to us. First, they would force you to do something like dig a trench or wash their clothes. If you said no, they'd say you were rude and beat you up. They told us, "This is not a Holiday Inn." They swore at us. Once three or four detainees were forced to dig a big hole. They had no water to drink and became very thirsty. The guards said, "Call Nujoma to come help you, he's your god." We asked Commander Leicher, "How long will we be held?" He said, "The public is afraid of you." He was very sly. He would order soldiers to disrupt our beds, pour cold water on us. He ordered them to do that but then he acted very sympathetic toward us.[15]

A female detainee, Amalia Aupindi, described the Mariental camp as being completely overgrown and filled with snakes. The detainees had to sleep in tents and only later on was some

---

[14] Soggot, *The Violent Heritage*, p. 288.

[15] Africa Watch interview with Willie Amutenya, Katutura, April 1991.

form of prefabricated housing constructed for them. The detainees had to sleep on the floor because there were no beds for them.[16]

According to Pineas Aluteni who was held at the camp, the conditions were especially primitive when they first arrived. They were threatened by guards who made use of the camp's secret status:

> We were divided into tents that had been put up in the grass—no beds but everyone was given two filthy blankets like those in prisons.

> A Boer lieutenant welcomed us by saying that he was happy to have us there but he would not tolerate any SWAPO shit. He further told us that we could be shot there and thrown away like dogs as nobody knew where we were.

Conditions inside Mariental were miserable:

> We had our meal once a day that consisted of one unpeeled potato each and five tins of corned beef that had to be boiled in a pot of water in order to be shared by about 140 people.

> We were subjected to hard labor such as digging trenches, removing stones from the camp, erecting guard towers. Sometimes we were made to run while carrying sandbags.

> It was terrible—nobody was allowed to move at night even to go to the toilet but luckily the one peeled potato helped us not to need a toilet so regularly. There were four or five roll calls every night and imagine how cold it is in the south. We were not given any clothes, not to speak of shoes and thus many of us had to walk on hands and feet in the thorns and stones. The one potato supper went on until mid-September.

> Some days we refused to work and as punishment we would not have supper. We were not allowed to keep any books, a paper or a pen and [there was] no communication with the outside world. A pencil or a piece of paper found in the camp could mean losing two suppers.

> Our toilets were just something like a shallow well and when it became full we had to scoop out all the rubbish with buckets and pour it into a municipal truck from Mariental. This meant that the whole camp smelt of shit on the day of cleaning the toilets and this can be confirmed by the ICRC delegates.

---

[16] Gwen Lister, "The Cassinga Detainees: The Case of Amalia Aupindi," A Paper Presented to The UN Council For Namibia Symposium on "A Century of Heroic Struggle of the Namibia People Against Colonial Occupation," November 1984.

According to Aluteni, prisoners were beaten outside the camp in a secluded valley:

Physical assaults were conducted in a valley outside the camp. Anyone found to disobey the orders of the camp had to be taken out by a group of soldiers and in the valley such a comrade was attacked by the Boers as if by a group of hungry wolves.[17]

Achille Angulla was also a prisoner at the Mariental camp. He described how the guards used simulated executions to intimidate the prisoners:

To play with our feelings they would take a colleague out of the camp. You would hear a shot. They would tell us, "We'll shoot you too." Then the guy would come back later on, beaten up.

Willie Amutenya described an incident where he narrowly escaped a beating or worse:

I wore a black power shirt with a raised fist. I was told, "That's instigating." I told them, "Your uniform insults me." In the night I was taken out by three soldiers but I was saved by a lieutenant of the troops that we played soccer with. He knew me as a good guy.

Starting in 1981, South Africa permitted the ICRC to visit the prisoners every three months. The head of the ICRC mission in Pretoria, Andre Coulomb, stated that the ICRC regarded the Mariental detainees as prisoners of war entitled to the protections of the Third Geneva Convention of 1949. As such, hard labor like road construction and tree clearing they were required to perform violated the Geneva Convention norms on the treatment of prisoners of war.[18] The visits by the ICRC had a marked effect on the treatment of the detainees:

There was a period when no one knew where we were. The ICRC came in 1980. When we were still at Oshakati we managed to collect everybody's name and they were smuggled out to Geneva. Once we stole a newspaper and we saw that our names had reached Amnesty International and later we learned that the ICRC would visit us. Things changed a bit before the ICRC visit. We got better food and blankets.

---

[17] Speech by Pineas Aluteni on the Tenth Anniversary of the Assault on Kassinga Camps, Windhoek, reprinted by the Namibia Communications Centre, May 4, 1988.

[18] Allister Sparks, "Pretoria Thwarts Suit Seeking Release of Prisoners in Namibia," *The Washington Post*, May 3, 1984, p. A26.

We had a committee to meet with the ICRC when they visited. That helped because the soldiers couldn't attack us. There had been rumors of plans to scatter us but once the ICRC arrived they couldn't do that.[19]

On March 6, 1984, a law suit was filed to force the release of the Mariental prisoners. According to David Smuts, one of the lawyers, its purpose was to challenge "the legality of the Army capturing these people in a foreign country, abducting them across an international border and holding them prisoner indefinitely."[20] In an affidavit Smuts stated:

The . . . captives have been removed from the sovereign state of Angola, held against their will in captivity for nearly six years, denied their common law rights, not least to liberty, and have not been charged or brought to trial in all that time. It also appears that in certain instances, there has been maltreatment, unlawful under both the laws of this Territory and international law.[21]

In May 1984, just prior to the court date scheduled to hear the case, the South African Minister of Justice, Kobie Coetsee, issued an order which halted the proceedings in the "national interest."[22] Mr. Coetsee was authorized to take such action by Section 103 of South Africa's Defence Act. This section deals with court cases against the state, the President, the Minister of Defence or any other public servant. If the law suit was directed against an action taken by any official in good faith while preventing terrorism, the Minister of Justice could issue a certificate halting legal proceedings. The Minister was not required to give reasons for his intervention and Coetsee did not give any. The law did not allow an appeal of the Minister's decision. Shortly afterwards, a group of detainees were released from Mariental. By October 1984, the last Mariental prisoners were freed.

In May 1984, Achille Angulla was released. In Windhoek he learned how dangerous the situation had become in the north.

At the time of my release, Captain Coetsee was the camp commander. We were photographed for identification. We were told we would be released. We were driven by lorry to Windhoek and received there by the Council of Churches in Namibia (CCN). We were also given accommodations by the CCN. This was in May 1984. We were told that we were no longer being held because the time had

---

[19] Africa Watch interview with Willie Amutenya, Katutura, April 1991.

[20] Allister Sparks, "Pretoria Thwarts Suit Seeking Release of Prisoners in Namibia," *The Washington Post*, May 3, 1984, p. A26.

[21] Lister, *The Cassinga Detainees*, quoting affidavit of David Smuts.

[22] "South Africa Blocks Court Action Aimed At Freeing Namibia Rebels," *New York Times*, May 2, 1984.

come to bring us before the court. I was warned by the CCN not to go to the north. They told me that things were different there from what they had been when we lived there.

Willie Amutenya was held for six additional months and sent to a special indoctrination center in an effort to win him away from SWAPO. The center was run by a special group called Etango. One detainee described Etango as "part of Koevoet. They go on patrols with Koevoet, in the same cars, with the same guns and the same uniforms." When released he had to leave the north because of the dangers posed by Koevoet. According to Amutenya:

When the first group was released we had hoped that we would be released very soon. But nothing happened. We were sent to Etango, whose aim was to win our "hearts and minds." Etango was a cultural group, really a brainwashing program against communism. They preached the gospel of free enterprise. We left Mariental and were taken to "Meerswoop" which means "ant hill." The purpose of going there was to be given certain courses to make you hate SWAPO and support their system. Etango was affiliated with the Broderbond of South Africa. We were released on October 18, 1984. There was a ceremony. The Etango group was very bitter, because no one who was released joined their group. We had to leave the north because it was very dangerous there, so we came back to Windhoek. The situation had changed due to Koevoet.

5. VIOLENCE AGAINST THE CIVILIAN POPULATION OF THE NORTH

LEGAL STANDARDS

Africa Watch evaluates the conduct of the South African military and security forces towards civilians in Namibia by the standards of international humanitarian law which apply to armed conflicts between the military forces of different countries as well as to armed conflicts between government forces and insurgent groups.

In 1968, the South African Mandate over Namibia was revoked by the United Nations General Assembly; the following year, the Security Council formally recognized this change of status. On June 21, 1971, the International Court of Justice (ICJ) declared South Africa's presence in Namibia unlawful. Under international law, therefore, Pretoria's continued rule there was an illegal occupation. The end of the Mandate and the ICJ ruling transformed the nature of the armed conflict between South Africa's military and SWAPO under the laws of war. No longer an internal conflict, it became an international one.

As a consequence of these developments, South Africa's conduct must be analyzed under the rules of international armed conflict. In such conflicts, the Geneva Conventions of 1949 are the principal applicable provisions of law, especially the Fourth Geneva Convention, which concerns the treatment of civilians.[1]

Like almost every government in the world, South Africa is a state party to the 1949 Geneva Conventions. The Convention contains a number of provisions dealing with occupied territories. Article 27, which sets forth the duties of an occupying power, requires that "protected persons . . . shall at all times be humanely treated, and protected especially against all acts of violence or thereof . . . ." It states that "Women shall be especially protected against any attack on their honor, in particular against rape . . . or any form of indecent assault." Article 31 prohibits "physical or moral coercion . . . against protected persons, in particular to obtain information from them or third parties." Article 32 prohibits any measure that would cause "physical suffering or extermination of protected persons . . . . This prohibition applies not only to murder, torture, corporal punishment, mutilation . . . but also to any other measures of brutality whether applied by civilian or military agents." Article 33 bars collective punishment.

---

[1] In 1977, Protocol I to the Geneva Conventions was adopted. Protocol I specifically governs "armed conflicts in which peoples are fighting against colonial domination and alien occupation and against racist regimes in the exercise of their right of self-determination . . . ." The war in Namibia falls into this category. South Africa, however, is not a party to Protocol I and only such provisions of the Protocol as are also customary international law govern its behavior. However, the Fourth Geneva Convention contains specific protections for the civilian population which clearly apply to South Africa's conduct.

The Fourth Geneva Convention reinforces these prohibitions by requiring that an occupying power investigate and punish those responsible for serious violations. Article 146 requires a state to enact legislation necessary to provide penal sanctions for any person committing "grave breaches." Article 147 defines "grave breaches" as "willful killing, torture or inhuman treatment . . . willfully causing great suffering or serious injury to body or health, unlawful deportation or transfer or unlawful confinement of a protected person . . . or willfully depriving a protected person of the rights of fair and regular trial." States have a duty to search for persons who have committed or who were ordered to commit grave breaches and bring them to prosecution. Thus, there are clear standards by which to assess South African conduct.

As the war intensified in Namibia, the north came under extensive military occupation by a number of South African military and security forces. Encouraged by comprehensive security legislation and unrestrained by virtually any controls, these forces were responsible for a pattern of indiscriminate violence against the civilian population, including: arbitrary arrests; widespread torture during interrogation; long term detention without charge or trial; disappearances; and summary executions.

ARBITRARY ARRESTS

In the late 1970s, the South African authorities enacted regulations which provided the legal authority for arbitrary arrests. The Security Districts Proclamation of 1977 (widely known as AG 9) authorized the security forces to arrest and detain incommunicado a person for interrogation for 96 hours. The authorized period of incommunicado detention was later extended by amendment to thirty days. The language of AG 9 allowed the broadest discretion in making an arrest:

> A commissioned or non-commissioned officer of the security forces, who suspects that any person who is within a security district, committed an offence at any time, or intends or at any time intended to commit an offence or is in possession of information relating to the commission of an offence by any person or any person's intention to commit an offence, may without a warrant arrest a person and for the purpose of interrogation, order him to be detained.

Once in custody, the detainee was not allowed to consult with a lawyer except with the approval of the Administrator General. The Administrator General could extend the initial thirty day period indefinitely.

The Detention for the Prevention of Political Violence and Intimidation Proclamation, (AG 26 of 1978) empowered the Administrator General to order the arrest and detention of any person he deemed to be obstructing or hindering "peaceful and orderly constitutional development" in Namibia through violence or intimidation.

In practice, individuals were repeatedly arrested because they were SWAPO members or because they were believed to be SWAPO supporters. Others were arrested because they had participated in peaceful activities deemed subversive by the authorities. Those arrested under these Proclamations were not allowed access to family members or lawyers, nor informed of charges against them and, in most cases, were not formally charged with an offense under the criminal law. After a period of time, they were generally released from custody.

Africa Watch interviewed a SWAPO member who lived in Katutura township outside Windhoek. In 1984, she was repeatedly arrested by the South African security forces, held incommunicado in solitary confinement and then released without ever being charged. Her first arrest occurred because she was handing out invitations for a SWAPO barbecue at her home.[2] She told Africa Watch:

> My first arrest was in 1984 when I was 26 years old. I never had an encounter with the police before that time. I was arrested because after the clampdown in 1978 we [the local SWAPO activists] were re-activating and re-structuring ourselves. At the time we were having a barbecue at my house and I was arrested for that. I was a nurse at Katutura Hospital and I was arrested wearing my hospital uniform. I was passing out papers, invitations, on the bus on the way to work. The South African security police at the gate got hold of one of the invitations and then they came for me. The officer said, "I am looking for you." I said, "this is for a barbecue." He said, "This is a SWAPO thing."

> I was first taken to security headquarters in Windhoek and then removed to Okahandja without any notification to my family. That was when I first realized how my rights were being violated. I stayed in a cell by myself, talking to myself.

To press the authorities to allow her to see a lawyer, she refused food. At one point she was beaten by relatives of the prison guards and told that they had her young son in custody. She was released after a few weeks:

> They said that I was very hard. They were accusing me of holding meetings, claiming that they had information from "Person B." I said, go and call "Person B" so I can contradict him. After two days of being in the cells I decided that I was not going to eat. On the night of the third day the brothers of some of the police came to the cell where I was being held to beat me and insult me. I just took water because I wanted a lawyer and I wanted my family to bring me things. I tried to make myself used to the cell, to pass time in the cell. There would be

---

[2] During the years of South African rule SWAPO was not legally banned by the colonial authorities. There was an internal SWAPO structure which organized activities inside Namibia while the external wing carried on armed conflict. The internal SWAPO leadership explained that there were two wings with the same objectives, "only the means are different."

children crying in other cells. They would tell me this was my son. I said, "it's not my son, he doesn't cry like that."

I stayed in Okahandja for two weeks and then I was transferred to Windhoek where I was released on April 27, 1984.

Her second arrest occurred at a picnic celebrating the release of Namibian political prisoners from Robben Island:

At the time of my second arrest in June 1984, I was working for the Catholic Social Services in Katutura. The Namibian prisoners had just been released from Robben Island and Mariental. We were going to have a party in the bush. We had posters, t-shirts. There were soldiers in camouflage there already. It was just a social day. We were preparing the picnic and the soldiers surrounded us and arrested us. I was taken from Dordabis to Windhoek. We were transferred in the middle of the night—they did that so people wouldn't know where their comrades were. I was held for five days and then released. We were to appear in court in September. It was postponed and we were arrested [again] during a demonstration outside the courthouse.

Africa Watch interviewed Onesmus Nekondo, who was born in Ombalantu and raised in the north. He worked as a contract laborer in Okahandja and later served as an assistant teacher until 1988. In 1989, he went to work full time for the Justice and Peace Commission of the Roman Catholic Church. He was arrested several times and held for months by the security forces in the north without being notified of any charges:

I was held for a month without even being told why I was there. In April 1982, after six months I was released without anything being said. I was not even given the reason why I was arrested.

In July 1982, I was arrested again. That time I was held for two days at Mahane. I was not told why I was being detained. I was asked questions about the guerrilla movement. When they got no satisfactory answer I was released.

Suspected SWAPO supporters were frequently arrested and detained if some act of property destruction occurred. According to Nekondo:

If you had a contact with SWAPO, you were always a target. If something was damaged like a telephone pole, they would come to you. I can remember one man detained several times: Fabian Andjawba. Fabian was arrested many times. He was not able to endure this kind of treatment. He left Namibia to go into exile in 1987.

Heike Sliufa was a Robben Island prisoner who was arrested and held many times in the Osire camp [a secret detention center]. I know of people like Bertinus Namandi who was a victim of detention several times. He was tortured and beaten for being a suspected SWAPO supporter.

Involvement in any kind of protest was grounds for arrest. On October 19, 1977, at the Government School in Ongwediva, a dispute arose between students and the head of the school over the wearing of school uniforms. The students also complained about corporal punishment at the school, and a number of students were ordered to leave the campus. Seven of them were told that they could not return without submitting to a beating; the remainder left in protest. Following that action, a number of the students at the Ongwediva School were arrested. According to Hosea Mbandeka, one of those arrested:

> On October 28, I received a report that members of the South African Army had been to my home and left a message that I was to go to the Security Branch offices at Oshakati.

> In response to the message I went to the office of the Security Branch of the South African Police . . . on the same day, the 28th October 1977. I was arrested and placed in a cell. Prior to being put in the cell I was searched and my belongings taken from me. I asked why I was being arrested and was told that I was being arrested for what I had done at school. I was not told, however, what crime I had committed.[3]

Mbandeka was tortured during interrogation and released several weeks later without charge.

Sakeus Shivute, at the time a twenty-two-year-old student at the Ongwediva College, had a similar experience after the school walkout. He received a message the Security Police were looking for him and that he was to report to their offices:

> A dispute arose between the students and the head of the college, Mr. Bouwer, and as a result of that dispute a number of students, including myself, were expelled. When I was expelled, I went home to Oshigambo.

> Towards the end of October, a few days after I had left the school, I received a message to say that five members of the Security Branch of the South African Police Force had called at my house and were looking for me. They had left a message saying that I was to come to their office on the following Monday.

---

[3] Affidavit of Hosea Mbandeka, filed in the case *Franciscus Petrus v. The Minister of Police and Colonel Schoon*, reprinted in H. Hunke and J. Ellis, eds., *Torture—a cancer in our society*, (Windhoek: Self-Published, 1977) p. 75.

On the following Monday, i.e. Monday the 31st October 1977, I went to the Security Branch office at Oshakati. When I arrived there I was arrested and put in detention in the army camp at Oshakati.[4]

Shivute was interrogated about the circumstances of the walk-out at the college and brutally tortured. He too was released two weeks later without charge.

INTERROGATION AND TORTURE

Koevoet and the Security Police, routinely abused detainees to extract information about SWAPO or the movement and whereabouts of PLAN combatants. The testimony of victims makes clear that the use of torture by the South African forces was commonplace.

Africa Watch interviewed Erastus Uutoni, whose *nom de guerre* was "Napoleon." Uutoni now works at the Human Rights Centre in Ongwediva. He was arrested by two Ovambo members of Koevoet in a bar in Oshakati on January 24, 1985, after a PLAN fighter had been captured and had given information incriminating Uutoni. The latter was ordered at gunpoint to go to the security force station in Oshakati where the captured PLAN member was held and then interrogated, beaten and tortured with an electric shock machine until he lost consciousness. Uutoni's experiences at several different Koevoet bases and detention sites demonstrate how widely torture was used and how detainees were shifted back and forth between Koevoet, the para-military force, and the Security Police:

DuPlessis, a member of the SADF, joined Nicky and Matias, the Ovambo officers who arrested me. DuPlessis asked me for my ID card and then he asked me if I was "Napoleon." This was a name during the struggle. I denied it. They started laughing. They asked me if I knew the guy who had been beaten and was chained to the table. I denied that I knew the man. They insisted that I was Napoleon. "He is your comrade and he told us everything. It won't help if you deny it."

After that I was taken to another place. DuPlessis was accompanied by another white man, a member of the security forces. They started asking me about the man chained to the table and about some war materials that were brought in some time ago. I denied all this and they started beating me with their fists. They tore my shirt off and blindfolded with me with it. They drew my belt off and bound my hands behind my back. When they finished they started beating me again. They brought the electric shock machine in and started giving me electric shocks all over my body. They continued with beatings and electric shocks up till the time that I became unconscious. They told me that I must talk.

---

[4] Affidavit of Sakeus Shivute, reprinted in Hunke and Ellis, eds., *Torture*, p. 29.

They took me back to the same place and left two black members of the security forces to guard me. During that night I was lying on the floor, they came back and beat me and poured cold water all over my body.

I was taken to Ondangwa police station, where they kept me without food or water. Then they took me back to the Oshakati police station where the beatings and electric shock was the food of the day and night, day and night, day and night.

Uutoni's mistreatment reveals how responsibility for the inhumane treatment extended to the highest echelons of the security forces. At one point Uutoni's questioning was conducted by the chief of interrogation of the Security Police, Colonel Gerrit Badenhorst, who was based in Windhoek. Badenhorst threatened him with death and began to beat him:

Colonel Badenhorst came to Oshakati to see me. Colonel Badenhorst started telling me that I must give a full statement that is true and that if he found out that what I told him was not true, I would be beaten to death. So I gave him a statement of maybe ten lines. Maybe he thought that it wasn't true. He started beating me with his fists.

Brutal treatment was not limited to detainees. According to testimony from Uutoni, the beating of his relatives, a form of collective punishment, was also sanctioned by the senior leadership of the South African security forces. He told Africa Watch that a leading officer in the Security Police, Colonel Nel, authorized the beating of his father, mother and sister as well as the destruction of their home:

They put me . . . in a landrover and chained [me] in. They covered me with blankets and told me to lie down on the floor while they jumped on my body. We left, but I don't know where I was taken to. There were several of us in the landrover. We were blindfolded and chained together and told to follow the person in front of us. I was taken back to Oshakati. Captain Ballach and Colonel Nel were there . . . the top of the South African forces. They told us that our homes would be destroyed and we were waiting for the Casspirs [South African armored personnel carriers] to arrive. The Casspirs arrived and took me to my home.

I found my mother beaten and lying on the ground. My father was beaten and lying on the ground, as was my sister. I was chained before my mother and father and beaten and kicked. As we left, the Casspirs arrived along with bulldozers. They destroyed the fields . . . nothing was left. We never got anything for what we lost. The whole place was destroyed.

The abuse endured by Uutoni apparently reflected his captors' dissatisfaction with statements he gave them. His experiences at camps in Oshikuku and Oniimwandi in Oshakati illustrate the pervasiveness of torture by the security forces:

Afterwards I was taken to Oshikuku. I was chained in the Casspir and a certain captain who had been cross-examining me started to beat me, accusing me of making [a] false statement to the magistrate in Windhoek and Colonel Badenhorst.

The purpose of such beatings was to damage certain internal organs so that you could die at any time. You would be released and then die after several months. They knew exactly that if they beat you in a certain organ you would die.

I was taken back to Oniimwandi, a Koevoet camp in Oshakati. Many atrocities were committed there. I was taken from solitary confinement to Captain Ballach's office. Ballach was there along with four white men and a black officer named "Tjako," a nickname. They tied me to a long iron. They handcuffed me. They suspended me, blindfolded me so I couldn't see who was beating me. They got an electric machine. They beat me and gave me electric shock. Beatings and electric shocks were a daily practice. This went on for maybe three weeks.

At a certain point Uutoni was taken out into the bush, suspended from a tow truck and given electric shocks while security officers sat eating and drinking below:

After that they organized a barbecue—they called it "Napoleon's *Braaivleis*." I was taken out of the cell to a place where I still don't know where it was. At this place I was chained with handcuffs behind my back. My legs were chained. They took strong rope and tied it behind my back and I was lifted up by a tow truck. I was only able to see the ground. They took two electric machines. They took my penis out of my pants. They poured cold water all over my body and gave me electric shocks all over. They put the electric shocks on my private parts. They said, "Now we are enjoying Napoleon's Braaivleis."

They asked me if I had children and said that I would never see my children again. They said to me, "We have mistreated you and we are going to kill you and hide your body so no one will find it. So you will know about Koevoet and you will disappear." They had a braai [braaivleis]. I heard them sitting, eating and drinking. At that time I couldn't feel anything in my body below the arms. I was beaten and had shocks on my ears and neck. When they became tired I was taken back to the camp at Oniimwandi.

Another security force captain made him hold his arms upright while bricks were tied to his hands:

A captain from Oshakati would take me to a certain place where they tied bricks on your hands, making you hold the bricks up. When you became tired they would beat you with a hose pipe. If you lowered your arms, they would beat you on the elbow. With the bricks, you would stand there the whole night, watched by two guards. There was another tactic that they would use. They would beat you on your anklebone with an iron stick or they would use a pliers to pull out a toenail.

The torture was facilitated by the maintenance of secret detention camps. In 1982, reports emerged that detainees were being held for interrogation at a secret center run by the Security Police at Osire, near the farming hamlet of Hochveld, 120 kilometers north of Windhoek. Reportedly, detainees were blindfolded while in the presence of their interrogators, systematically beaten with a flexible pipe, tortured by electric shock, beaten on the naked buttocks with a thick plank and kept in solitary confinement. They were coerced into signing statements that they had not read in advance.[5]

As deputy chief of the Security Police, Colonel Gerrit Badenhorst, had overall responsibility for interrogation of detainees, including responsibility for Osire. According to Erastus Uutoni:

They finished their investigation and we were taken to Osire Camp, ten kilometers from Otjiwarongo. The Osire Camp was deep in the forest—no one knew the place existed, only the security forces. We called it a second Robben Island.

At Osire I was kept in solitary confinement. I was told that I had no right to a lawyer. Later I learned that lawyers were prohibited from coming to see us.

I was taken to a building where there were many members of the security forces. Colonel Badenhorst, Nicky, Mathias. I was taken from my cell to a place where I was cross-examined by guards with guns. You were forced to talk. If you didn't you would be beaten by them.

Unlike many of those arrested by the security forces, Uutoni was later charged with a specific criminal offense.

Then I was taken from Osire to Windhoek where I met several colonels who asked me about sabotage that I didn't know anything about. They took me with three policeman before a magistrate in Windhoek. I was told that I should await trial and was sent back to Osire.

---

[5] "Torture in Namibia," *South African Outlook*, April 1985, p. 58.

In 1986, Uutoni was tried and sentenced to twelve years in prison. He was released from Windhoek Central Prison with twenty other prisoners on July 20, 1989, under the terms of Resolution 435.

The procedures of the security forces that encouraged rampant torture were documented in testimony by officers in a publicized trial, *State v. Heita and Seven Others*.[6] Andreas Heita and seven other defendants were charged under the Terrorism Act No. 83 of 1967 for a bombing in Windhoek and the possession of explosives. The eight defendants had been arrested separately at various times and locations. At trial, the defense lawyer challenged the admissibility of confessions obtained during pre-trial detention on the grounds that they had been obtained by duress.[7] As a result, there was a "trial within a trial" over this evidentiary issue. This revealed the attitudes of the torturers.

Heita had sustained a gunshot wound in his arm at the time of his arrest. He was taken to a hospital facility where his arm was treated. An intravenous tube was placed in his other arm and he was then taken to a police station where he was interrogated by a Koevoet officer, Captain Franz Ballach.

Captain Ballach admitted freely during cross-examination that he had beaten Heita with a meter long hose pipe:

"Did you do anything to the accused during interrogation?"

"Yes I did."

"What did you do to him?'

"I hit him."

"With what?"

"With a piece of hose pipe."

"How long did the interrogation last?"

"About three hours."

Ballach acknowledged that he had assaulted Heita but he described the beating as harmless. Responding to a question by the court, he said to the judge, "Your Honor, I knew he

---

[6] *State v. Heita And Seven Others*, quoted in Hinz and Leuven-Lachinski, *Koevoet*, p. 28.

[7] Amnesty International, Annual Report, 1988, p. 60.

would not die. The kind of treatment that I gave him would definitely not kill him." Heita showed the court extensive scars on his head, back and shoulders that resulted from the beating.

In another exchange with the judge, Ballach justified his methods by claiming that the beating was necessary to prevent further assaults:

> "The sole reason why I did it was to prevent assaults that might become too harsh."

> "Did you think that if you did not hit him others might then hit him even harder?"

> "They might, Your Honor, and things may run out of hand when more people start hitting."

Other security officers who testified admitted that they believed it was necessary to utilize "maximum violence" to obtain "satisfactory information" from detainees. One officer with thirteen years' service testified that officers were permitted to use any means necessary to obtain information so long as they did not "unnecessarily" kill detainees.

In an exchange with the judge, Ballach revealed that Koevoet did not maintain records of the prisoners it had interrogated:

> Your Honor, we in Koevoet do not keep records. If records must be kept, this should have been the duty of the police investigator.

Following this testimony, the defendants' self-incriminating statements obtained as a result of beatings were withdrawn by the state; even so, six of eight defendants were convicted.[8] The court severely condemned the beatings, characterized the interrogations as "brutal assaults," and urged that Captain Ballach be prosecuted. It transferred the case to the Attorney General who subsequently announced that there would be no prosecution.[9]

Beatings were routinely administered by Koevoet officers in the effort to extract incriminating information about suspected PLAN fighters. On November 28, 1986, in the town of Oitende, near the Angolan border, Reuben Edmund and Andreas Abisai were walking along a road when they saw a number of Casspirs moving towards them. Recognizing that the Casspirs belonged to Koevoet, they ran off in different directions. Andreas was pursued and apprehended. The Koevoet officers tried to force him to admit that Reuben Edmund was a PLAN combatant:

---

[8] Ibid.

[9] Hinz and Leuven-Lachinski, *Koevoet*, pp. 27–29.

The . . . security force members then proceeded to question me about [Reuben], asking whether I knew him and where he worked. They said that they had apprehended and detained him. They also asked me whether he was a trained insurgent of SWAPO's military wing which I emphatically denied. When I denied this, the . . . security force members repeatedly beat me with sticks on my back and on my buttocks. They . . . dug a hole and forced my head into it, covering my head with sand so that I felt that I was about to suffocate. During these assaults . . . I was continually blindfolded.[10]

Following this, Andreas was transported to the base at Outapi and then to another base at Rucana where the torture continued:

On the following day, I was conveyed to a security force base at Rucana where I was kept in detention until I was released on 3 December 1986. During my detention at Rucana, security force members blindfolded me and interrogated me about [Reuben] . . . they severely assaulted me by beating me with a hosepipe and whips . . . .[11]

Onesmus Nekondo identified yet another base as a torture center. He told Africa Watch:

I was detained in March 1982 for the first time in the Ovamboland area. For a long time I was searched and questioned.

I was taken to a military base at Mahanae. There I was severely tortured with electricity and beaten to [make me] agree that I had helped SWAPO fighters. The following day I was taken to Ogongo. Then I was transferred to the Oshakati Detention Camp. There were many people there and the camp was divided into two parts: one for local people arrested as SWAPO supporters and another for captured guerrilla fighters.

The use of torture was not limited to Koevoet. The Security Police, whose role pre-dated Koevoet's formation, savagely abused detainees. Hosea Mbandeka, the student at the Ongwediva Government School who had been arrested for participating in the walkout of October 1977, was held for three days in a cell at the offices of the Security Police in Oshakati. Then he was blindfolded and driven into the bush. Mbandeka reported:

---

[10] Affidavit of Andreas Abisai, filed in *David Ekondo v. the Cabinet for the Interim Government and Another*, Windhoek Supreme Court (June 29, 1987), reprinted in Southern Africa Project, *Human Rights Violations in Namibia*, unpublished, (Washington: Lawyers' Committee for Civil Rights Under Law).

[11] Ibid.

I walked a short distance and was led up two steps, into what I presume was a building. I was then made to sit down on a chair and my hands were tied behind the chair. My feet were also tied together. A rope was also put around my body, securing me to the back of the chair. An object was then put against my forehead, above my left eye, and something which felt like a cloth, was then wound around my head, pressing the object against my forehead. Water was then thrown onto my head and forehead on the side where the object had been placed. My trousers were also pulled down to my knees and something which felt like a clip, attached to my genitalia. The white officer then said,"Today we are going to talk." He asked why I had left the college. I said that I had left because of the way in which students were treated. I said the beating of students was inhuman. I then heard what sounded like the whine of a machine and felt a sudden violent sensation in my head which I believed to be electric shock. It seemed to kick my head upwards. I could not breath. I felt confused and frightened and felt my head was breaking into fragments.

At the same time I felt an agonizing burn in my testicles. The burning pain ran through my legs and also went into my stomach. My whole body was jumping. The White officer said that they would burn me in this fashion until my "gat" was broken. When the burning stopped my jaws shut violently together so that I bit my tongue repeatedly and it bled. I was also interrogated as to who had tried to set fire to the mattress room at the college. I replied that I had no idea. I said that had happened when I was already back at home. Not satisfied with this, I was burnt again and again, the officer insisting that I knew the names of the people who had set alight the college.[12]

This treatment continued as Mbandeka's interrogators demanded the names of the students who had led the walk-out at the school. He was given electric shocks again and asked for his membership card in SWAPO. He replied that he was not a member.

Later, he was taken back to the Security Police offices in Oshakati, where he gave a statement to the white officer who had participated in the interrogation. Mbandeka, whose tongue was swollen from biting it during electric shock, remained in custody until November 16, 1977, when he was released and allowed to return home. He was not charged. Two days later he went to the Onandjokwe Hospital for bleeding in the area of his genitals.

Lameke Iithete was a fifty-year-old farmer in 1977 living at Ongandjera, at Okahao with his wife and two children. On May 4, 1977, he was arrested by a lieutenant of the Security Police and taken to a military camp at Oshakati where he was held for nearly two weeks. Shortly after his arrest he was taken to the offices of the Security Police in Oshakati and given electric shock.

---

[12] Affidavit of Hosea Mbandeka, reprinted in Hunke and Ellis, eds., *Torture*, pp. 25–26.

I was taken to a building near the old Police station, where I was interrogated by a White officer . . . .A Black policeman of the Security Branch, namely Eino Johannes, was with him. I was then interrogated [about] my contact with the SWAPO branches in Walvis Bay and Windhoek. They also interrogated me on my sale of SWAPO membership cards.

Not satisfied with my explanations as to my contact with other SWAPO branches, the police officers . . . then took me into a room in the buildings. The door was closed behind me. I noticed that there were dark blankets hung over the windows. I was told to stand against a plank to which my body was tied. My arms were then tied to an iron rod which was behind me. My arms were outstretched, and once tied, I could not move away. I also noticed an object which appeared to be some sort of machine, with wires attached to it, in the corner of the room. While I was being tied, Eino Johannes said: "we are tying you, and then you are going to talk." I was afraid, because I did not know what was going to happen to me.

Eino Johannes then tied a cloth around my head, knotting it beneath my chin. He then tied another cloth, with a knot in it, in such a way that the knot was placed in my mouth. This cloth was tied behind my head. I was then blindfolded. The White officer then said to me: "Will you speak the truth?" I answered, "I have no truth to tell; I have already told the truth and have told you everything I know." Prior to being taken into the dark room I was warned by Eino Johannes that if I did not speak the truth, they would take me into the "donkerkamer" where I would be shocked.

A device was then applied to the left of my stomach and then another to the right of my stomach and then I suddenly felt a frightening, burning pain which went through my body, causing me to shake uncontrollably. I screamed. The pain was burning and swift and my body quivered.

The pain was unbearable and seemed to go on for ever. My whole body seemed to be burning.

Still unsatisfied with my answers, they put electricity into my head, slightly in front of my ears. The pain in my head was agonizing and I screamed and cried . . . .I begged for mercy and pleaded with them to let me go and not to hurt me again. Pleading with them was to no avail. The interrogation continued and I was later shocked.[13]

---

[13] Affidavit of Lamek Iithete, Ibid., pp. 45–46.

After giving a statement to the Security Police, Iithete was released on July 26, 1977. He was never charged with a crime.

In 1977, Rauna Shimbode, a qualified Assistant Nurse was twenty-five years old. On April 15, 1977, she was arrested by Captain Nel of the Security Branch of the South African Police and was told it was because she "was a friend of the terrorists." At the time Rauna believed that she was pregnant. She was taken to the main police station in Windhoek and several days later transported to Oshakati, hundreds of kilometers to the north. At the offices of the Security Police, Rauna was interrogated by a black policeman. When she was unable to give him the answers he wanted, she was told that she would be taken to a place where people were made to talk. She was blindfolded and taken to another room in the same building:

> There were a number of people in the room and I gathered that they were White. Joseph [the black policeman who had interrogated her] put a block of ice in my mouth and a cloth was firmly tied around my mouth so that I was unable to open it.
>
> I was then suspended by my arms with my back against a wall and my arms above my head, tied individually to some object in such a manner that my feet were completely clear of the ground, and my full weight was carried by my wrists, which I subsequently ascertained had been tied to bars above the windows by two towels.
>
> The White people then questioned me, using Joseph as an interpreter . . . . I answered those questions which I could, but many questions were put to me which I was unable to answer.
>
> After my interrogation had continued for some time, I suddenly felt terrible pain and shaking and trembling through one side of my face and my whole body on that side but was not aware of what caused this. This lasted for a period which I estimate to be between one and two minutes and then suddenly stopped, whereupon I was told that if I did not talk I would be killed. I answered all the questions which were put to me in the affirmative as I did not wish to be subjected to further treatment of this nature, even though my answers were untrue. The people interrogating me told me that they were not satisfied, and I experienced the same pain and trembling and shaking as previously, but this time on the other side of my face and body.[14]

When she was returned to her cell at the offices of the Security Police, Rauna discovered she had serious vaginal bleeding. The floor of her cell was covered with blood. When she asked for a doctor, a man in a military uniform who said he was a doctor appeared and examined her.

---

[14] Affidavit of Rauna Shimbode, Ibid., p. 31.

He told her she had an infection and prescribed aspirin and an antibiotic. Several days later she was interrogated by a white officer, Van Niekerk, who struck her across the face when her answers were not satisfactory. She gave him a statement.

On May 10, 1977, a colonel told Rauna that she was free to go. She was not charged. She had to make her own way from Oshakati to Windhoek—480 kilometers. Rauna experienced vaginal bleeding for fifteen days after the first interrogation. Her menstrual cycle became highly irregular and she required ongoing medical care.[15]

Torture was not limited to those held under the proclamations authorizing detention without charge. The security forces interrogated and physically abused civilians who they happened to seize while on patrol. No matter how coincidental the circumstances of arrest torture was likely to occur. During 1986, young males apprehended by the security forces were particular targets.

On June 28, 1986, a Koevoet unit tracking PLAN fighters seized thirteen-year-old Titus Paulus. They interrogated him about the whereabouts of PLAN fighters. Paulus, an Amakali Primary School student, told the para-military forces that he knew nothing about the movements of SWAPO guerrillas. They grabbed him and repeatedly swung him back and forth over a fire. Paulus, who was from Onyanya in the Amutse area, was taken to Onandjokwe Lutheran Hospital, where he was treated for serious burns on his back.

Paulus said that on June 28, 1986, he went with a friend to Iithindi:

We noticed several Casspirs stopping next to the kraal with many camouflaged men following our footprints. They came straight to me and my friend and shouted that they have found the terrorists. Many makakunya seized me and asked me about SWAPO guerrillas. I told them that I knew nothing about such men . . . they accused me of lying. One slapped me in the face and pulled off my jersey to blindfold me while others kicked and pulled my testicles.

They then carried me into the *mahangu* [millet] field where I was held by my arms and legs over a fire, and they roasted my back for a long time.

I was screaming out with great pain and they threw me onto my back and left.

---

[15] Ibid., p. 33.

My friends helped me home and when we arrived my back was completely swollen with parts of the skin falling off. My mother immediately took me to the Onandjokwe Hospital.[16]

Paulus's mother, Mrs. Annah Johannes, confirmed this account in a separate statement to the authorities.

In June 1986, fifteen-year-old Portias Blasius, from Onhemba village near Ombalantu, was hospitalized for severe facial burns. A group of twelve soldiers had come to the *cuca* shop where he worked. In an effort to get information from him, the soldiers pressed Blasius' face against a pipe of hot steam coming from the back of their idling Buffel truck. According to the boy, the soldiers:

> grabbed and threw me into the Buffel truck and took me with them to an undisclosed place where they accused me of being a little, stupid SWAPO and asked me about SWAPO fighters.

> Some soldiers started to beat me up while others pulling my hair held my face against the exhaust pipe. Although I was screaming very loudly those merciless white devils did not care and even left me there in the bush with much pain.

A local businessman, Mr. John Andjamba, took Blasius to the hospital. The boy's medical records show that he suffered from second degree burns caused by gas from an exhaust pipe.[17] The two officers responsible were convicted of assault and fined R500 (200 dollars) each.[18]

In June 1983, Ndara Kapitango, a sixty-three-year-old inhabitant of Kavangoland, was "roasted" over hot coals by members of the South West Africa Territorial Force (SWATF) after his wife had been raped by the SWATF men. His injured arm was later amputated and he required extended hospital treatment for serious leg burns.[19] After many painful months in the hospital,

---

[16] Statement filed with the Chairman of the Ovambo Administration, Mr. Peter Kalangula, quoted in *The Namibian*, June 30, 1986.

[17] Chris Shipanga, "SWATF confirms incident and promises inquiry," *The Namibian*, June 13, 1986, p. 3.

[18] Amnesty International, Annual Report 1987, p. 83.

[19] Michael Hornsby, "Namibia soldiers 'roasted peasant,'" *The Times*, (London, U.K.), November 9, 1983.

he was released and died shortly afterwards. The SWATF men were fined R50 ($20 at the time).[20]

Many victims died in the course of interrogations. One widely known fatality involved forty-eight-year-old Frans Uapota. He was beaten to death by SADF soldiers on November 28, 1984, in the bottle store that he owned near Eembo in the Hangwena area of northern Namibia. At about 6:00 P.M. a patrol of soldiers suddenly arrived and ordered everybody in the store to lie down. According to Mrs. Victoria Mweuhanga, Uapota's wife, the soldiers then started "beating and kicking us. I noticed that they attacked my husband like a pack of wild dogs."[21] They beat him, kicked him and hit him with their rifle butts but Uapota did not fight back or say anything. They demanded to know the location of PLAN fighters and accused him of giving them drinks. When the attack ended, his wife saw him lying motionless on the ground. According to Mrs. Mweuhanga, the soldiers then attacked Mr. Nikolau Andjelu. Uapota and Andjelu were left behind as the soldiers took the others in the store away with them. They were not allowed to return until late that night.

The next day, at the insistence of the village Headman, police and army officers returned to the scene of the incident. At that point it was learned that Uapota had died the previous night as a result of the assault. According to Mrs. Mwuehanga, her husband had been "dragged for about 200 meters with something tied around his neck."

Such deaths occurred in random circumstances. Jakobus Jeremis reported the death of his brother, Fillipus Kapala, in similar circumstances:

> My brother . . . Fillipus Kapala had a cuca shop on his land at Onandova. On July 31, 1982, the police force arrived at his cuca shop in two vehicles. They were looking for a terrorist. They then started beating Fillipus, the owner of the cuca shop. They beat him on the cheek and kicked him in the abdomen. He—Fillipus—then died on Sunday August 1, 1982, at his home. His corpse was removed from his home by Ohangwena police. We do not know where he is buried.[22]

---

[20] "Ordeal By Fire," Episcopal Churchpeople for a Free Southern Africa, August 8, 1986.

[21] *The Namibian*, December 6, 1985.

[22] Complaint filed with the Ovambo Administration by Jakobus Jeremia, Ondangwa, August 9, 1982.

DISAPPEARANCES

The unchecked powers of the South African security forces, the lack of procedures for keeping records of detainees, the maintenance of secret detention camps and the absence of accountability through the courts resulted in many disappearances of those detained by the security forces. Karl Ndroma, a captured PLAN combatant, was held by Koevoet at its Oshakati detention center. Ndroma now works for the Human Rights Centre in Ongwediva. He told Africa Watch:

> The people killed by Koevoet were never reported. The Koevoet activities were really clandestine activities in which they killed civilians. The reason they killed civilians is because they were paid for killings by the body. The reason they didn't report the killings to the police was because of the clandestine nature of their activities. When people were arrested or captured, their capture was not officially reported to the police station. So if you disappeared, the only place your family could look for you was with Koevoet and they would deny everything.

In fact many prisoners disappeared from the Koevoet detention camp in Oshakati. The physical construction of the camp facilitated disappearances. Karl Ndroma explained to Africa Watch:

> The camp was surrounded by a huge mound of gravel and sand. The base was demarcated by corrugated iron so that you couldn't see the interrogation offices or the cells from the outside. We would get information on the number of people inside the cells—the people who took the food would tell us that the cells were full. To give you an idea of how dangerous the situation was, when people died during interrogation, they could be removed from the camp without any one else knowing . . . .

> People who did not cooperate with the interrogators would be taken out and told to run away. They would be shot and their corpses would be brought back to the base.

> I know of people who were with us in the detention camps. One guy, whose name was Junias, was taken out by a Koevoet patrol. They took him out as if they were going to recruit him. The same day they killed him. He was taken to the bush and told to run away to Angola. They gave the body to the SADF as someone killed as a terrorist. The people at the mortuary told us this.

> Another guy was hanged in his cell. There was a Koevoet farm near Tsuemb where guys were taken to work. One guy who was taken there quarreled with an officer and was sent back to the detention camp. When this guy came back from

Tsuemb, he didn't take the quarrel very seriously. They took him right into a cell. People in the camp saw officers moving around the cell and after a while they were called and told the guy had hanged himself in his cell. Later we were told to take this guy's body from the cell. Some were told to bury the body without informing his family.

At the secret detention camp, Osire, many people were held without their family's knowledge. Erastus Uutoni who had been held there told Africa Watch:

There were people held there we had been looking for. One guy, Lucas Nujoma, who was detained without trial. His family didn't know of his whereabouts for years. We found him there working the camps. Also a fellow named John from West Oshakati.

Another source, Onesmus Nekondo, told Africa Watch:

There are people I remember who were arrested who disappeared. Kalebe Shikale was arrested in 1978. There was no other reason for arresting him other than that he was a SWAPO supporter. He was kept at Otaapi military camp. No one knows if he was taken somewhere else. In those years it was very difficult because people had no place to report these things. So you could be taken and no one would be able to follow you. There was no opportunity to report to the police force . . . .

I myself know of the case of Petrus Sankarie which was taken up by Lorentz and Bone [a prominent Windhoek law firm that handled many human rights cases during the period]. He was arrested in 1987. Later on, information came out that Petrus and another detainee had been killed and the case was withdrawn. The family of this man suffered so much pain because he was the only breadwinner. Lorentz and Bone tried to launch an investigation. They found out which unit arrested him, and who was the group leader. He had been captured by Koevoet and killed like a dog. Leon Lotts and Piet Bower, members of Koevoet, were brought before the Court in Ondangwa. They admitted that they had killed the two because they were SWAPO fighters. Everyone went out to the site of the killings. One doctor was called in from Windhoek to go to the grave and do a post mortem. There were several items taken out of the grave: shoes, a belt and a necklace identified by Petrus' mother as her son's.

The Koevoet officers who were found to have murdered Sankarie were later granted amnesty by the Administrator General.

Families reported many disappearances to the Ovambo Administration in the early 1980s. Louise Likela documented the circumstances of the disappearance of her husband, Fillemon Kasita Kambundu, a school teacher:

> During January 1981, the police of Ondangwa came to my home looking for my husband named Fillemon Kasita Kambundu who was at that time doing some teaching at Oshikondilongo School. When he came from school we gave him the message that he must report to police at Ondangwa. On the 30th January, 1981, he reported to Ondangwa police who took him [into] custody.
>
> On January 31, 1981, I reported at the Ondangwa police station and I was told by the Ovambo policeman, Amon Asser Kanguluwe, that my husband was taken to Oshakati Hospital on January 30, 1981. Up to this day I do not know where my husband is.
>
> During February 1982, I made further inquiries at Oshakati jail and I was told that my husband Fillemon had disappeared from the jail. I am now in a great doubt about this because he was not a terrorist. He was a school teacher at Oshikondilongo at the time. Please assist me to make the whereabouts of my husband Fillemon Kasita Kambundu.[23]

Emilia Penohungi of Okafakekola, Ondangwa North East, pressed the local authorities to furnish information on the fate of her son, Josef Gabriel:

> I live in my own home in Omkunda known as Okafakekola, Ondanga area. My son named Josef Gabriel was arrested by the police in Oshakati in January 1980. They—the police arrested Josef Gabriel at a cuca shop at Onakanuan area where he was found enjoying some drinks. Josef was arrested, I think on January 29, 1980, because I was with him on New Year's day, that is January 1, 1980. He was not told the reason why the police were arresting him. He was arrested together with one teacher named Zachariah Adam of Okak Omulilo, Ondonga and Johannes David Ndjomba also of Okakfakekola, Ondonga.
>
> I want to be informed where my son Josef Gabriel is.[24]

Thomas Gebhard of the Ongandjera Tribal Area complained to the local authorities:

---

[23] Complaint by Louisa Likela filed with the Ovambo Administration, Ondangwa, August 11, 1982.

[24] Complaint by Emilia Penohungi filed with the Ovambo Administration, Ondangwa, June 22, 1982.

My brother named Elago Gebhard was arrested from his home by Ovambo policemen on August 23, 1981. Elago Gebhard's home is also in the Omkundaukuvu in the Ongandjera area. I do not know the reason why Elago was arrested.

The police at Oshakati told me that Elago Gebhard died on August 24, 1981. I do not know where Elago is buried.

No message was sent to our family that Elago was dead.

I want to know the cause of death.[25]

Africa Watch interviewed a woman who had worked as a social worker in Katutura during the independence struggle. She described an incident involving the disappearance of a mentally retarded young man that showed the futility of pressing the authorities for information. According to Lindi Kazombaue:

There was a mentally retarded person, about twenty-four years old, who looked after cattle. One day he disappeared. At first his parents didn't know what had happened to him. Then his name appeared on a list published by the Justice and Peace Commission as a "disappeared" person. They came to me and asked me to try to trace him. I was working as a social worker for the Catholic church in Katutura at that time. I went to the ICRC. They took the details but couldn't do anything. At that time, in 1986, if you were stopped by the SADF and didn't have identification, you were detained. Finally, I went with the parents to the Minister of Justice of the Interim Government. He said that he had no jurisdiction over SADF, that he couldn't ask them any questions. That was the end of it.

The case of Reuben Edmund, the man chased by the Koevoet Casspirs in Otende on November 28, 1986, when he was walking down the road with Andreas Abisai, shows the lengths to which the authorities went to cover up the fate of those who disappeared in custody. After his arrest, Reuben was never seen alive again. For months his family searched for him while the colonial regime's officials consistently denied any knowledge of his whereabouts.

A neighbor of Reuben's told his uncle, David Ekondo, that he had witnessed Reuben's capture by the Casspir pursuing him. He said that Reuben was "seriously assaulted by [the] security force members and then loaded into a Casspir and taken away." [26]

---

[25] Complaint by Thomas Gebhard filed with the Ovambo Administration, Ondangwa, July 12, 1982.

[26] Affidavit of David Ekondo, Southern Africa Project, *Rights Violations in Namibia*, unpublished.

Though Andreas Abisai did not actually see Reuben's arrest by the Koevoet troops in the pursuing Casspirs, he did see one of Reuben's shoes on the floor of a Casspir:

I saw one of Reuben Edmund's shoes in the Casspir military vehicle I was conveyed in . . . I saw [the] shoe under my blindfold lying loose in [the] Casspir and clearly recognized [it] as being one of the shoes which [Reuben] had worn that day . . . I can positively say so as I am a close friend . . . and specifically recall the distinctive blue running shoes he wore on November 28, immediately prior to his apprehension.[27]

The efforts of Reuben's uncle, David Ekondo, a teacher, to find Reuben were typical:

On 28 November 1986, returning home from my school, I saw a number of Casspirs of the security forces at a cuca shop near my home, at a place known as Ombandua. A White member of the security forces asked me in Afrikaans where my nephew was and what sort of employment he was engaged in. I [said] that he should be at home and that he did not work.

The officer continued to question Ekondo:

He asked me why [Reuben] ran away . . . I replied I did not know that he had "run away." I was . . . asked why [Reuben] did not have a "tribal identity card," commonly referred to as a *staamkart* . . . I stated that I knew that he had one and I was then asked why he did not have a *kopkaart*, a term used for the compulsory identity document. I stated that I knew that he did not have one at present, but that he had a receipt or slip which indicated that he had in fact applied for one or for a replacement to a missing identity card.

There were a number of security force members present at the cuca shop, who were conveyed in at least four Casspir military vehicles and I noted the inscription of "Zulu 5" on one of [the] Casspirs.

I . . . proceeded to my home and made various inquiries about Reuben, who was not at home then, nor has he returned home since.

I was informed by . . . Junius Auwanga, that Reuben was caught by security force members in a Casspir in the vicinity of his home approximately ten to fifteen kilometers from where [he] was originally chased. Junius Auwanga further informed me that [Reuben] was seriously assaulted by [the] security force members and then loaded into the Casspir and taken away . . . .

---

[27] Affidavit of Andreas Abisai, Ibid.

In the course of my inquiries . . . I was informed by Mr. Kautondokwa and . . . Ndeshitiila . . . that they were at the cuca shop at Ombanda prior to my arrival there . . . and were asked by security force members, who had brought [Reuben] to them and exhibited him to them and asked them whether they knew "this terrorist" . . . .Kautondokwa and Ndeshitiila informed me that they both immediately denied that [Reuben] was a terrorist.

On 29 November 1986, I proceeded to the Outapi tribal office of Ombalantu and approached the senior headman for Ombalantu, Mr. Oswin Mukulu, to inquire concerning [Reuben's] whereabouts with the authorities.

I was present when Mr. Mukulu made inquiries with the Police base at Outapi and [we] were informed by a member of the security forces that Andreas Abisai and [Reuben] were being detained by them . . . .We were further told that the security force members would question them and as soon as they had completed their interrogation, [Reuben] and Andreas Abisai could go home.

After [Reuben] had not been released by 9 January 1987, I [went] to Mr. Oswin Mukulu to [make] further inquiries. I then proceeded with Mr. Mukulu to the police base at Outapi, where we had previously made inquiries and a young white policeman informed us that he knew nothing of [Reuben].

When [Reuben] had not been released by late January 1987, I approached representatives of my church [Evangelical Lutheran Church in Namibia] . . . to take up the detention of [Reuben] and to do whatever they could to secure the release and safety of [Reuben] . . . .[28]

There followed a lengthy series of letters and meetings with the office of the government attorney. In June 1987, Reuben's uncle filed an urgent application asking for a show cause order as to why Reuben should not be released. A court appearance was scheduled for July 24, 1987. In the meantime, Reuben's attorney uncovered evidence that suggested Reuben had died on the day he was arrested. On July 16, 1987, a government attorney submitted an affidavit stating that a man who had died in custody on November 28, 1986, was in fact Reuben Edmund. A post-mortem medical exam revealed that Reuben had suffered multiple contusions and abrasions.[29]

On April 9, 1985, a mass grave was found near the Roman Catholic Church at Oshikuku. According to Bishop Bonifatius Haushiku of the Windhoek Diocese, Catholic sisters discovered eight bodies decomposing in a ditch near the mission site. Church authorities called the police

---

[28] Affidavit of David Ekondo, Southern Africa Project, *Rights Violations in Namibia*, unpublished.

[29] Southern Africa Project, *Rights Violations in Namibia*, unpublished.

to investigate, but they did not respond. The SADF was then notified, but no action was taken. The Catholic nursing sisters from Oshikuku Hospital called South African doctors at Oshikuku, but again there was no action. Meanwhile many people whose relatives had been abducted by the South African police had come by to try to identify the corpses. Finally on Friday April 12, a government bulldozer arrived and buried the bodies, ending efforts at identification.

Brigadier Hans Dreyer, head of Koevoet, confirmed that his men had shot and killed the Namibians found near the Roman Catholic Mission in Oshikuku. In a statement issued on April 17 from his office in Oshakati, Dreyer said:

> There were four bodies for which I take responsibility. The terrorists were killed by one of my teams in the Tsambi area and brought to Oshikuku for identification. My men were told to bury the corpses but they must not have done a proper job. The bodies were not ditched but only buried under shallow soil.[30]

The assertion that the victims were "terrorists" was contradicted by Oswald Shivute, a former member of the Ovambo administration. In an interview with Africa Watch, Shivute said:

> There was an empty base near there. One evening Koevoet arrested people and brought them to the old base. People in the neighborhood could hear them crying. Koevoet shot them. They dug shallow graves. In the morning the dogs started eating the bodies. The stench filled the air when you drove by. There were more than five, mostly men.

BOMBINGS

The bank bombing in Oshakati on February 19, 1988 (see Chapter 2), was the most deadly but hardly the first such bombing in the north. Less than a year earlier, in April 1987, there had been bombings and arson attacks on at least fourteen schools, a clinic and a post office in northern Namibia. Residents claimed that South African security force members were involved. In one such incident, at Okambembe, one of five alleged saboteurs was shot and wounded by a civilian. Police from the Omungwelumwe Base arrived shortly after the shooting and allegedly identified the wounded man as a member of their unit.[31] They demanded to know why and by whom the man had been shot. Footprints of the saboteurs led from the Omungwelumwe Base to the site of the explosion. According to a source at the Ovambo Administration office, these footprints, which matched those found at several other schools that were destroyed, were pointed out to Chief Inspector Visser of Ondangwa. Live bullets and spent

---

[30] "South African Koevoet police admit killing 4 at Catholic mission in Namibia," *Namibian Communications Centre Telex*, April 17, 1985.

[31] Chris Shipanga, "Saboteurs target schools in Northern area," *The Namibian*, May 1, 1987. p. 4.

cartridges, apparently of South African origin, that were found at the scene were also shown to Inspector Visser.

On April 10, 1987, there was an explosion at the Omutundungu School. Prior to the blast, the principal, Mrs. Penelope Shikongo, said soldiers had come and broken the doors of two classrooms. After the explosion, a soldier who came to investigate identified the footprints as coming from military boots. They then removed a bomb that they identified as South African in origin.[32]

Churches were also targeted. According to Onesmus Nekondo:

On September 17, 1987, a Sunday, the Roman Catholic church at Omuulukila was blown up in the evening. I worked there as a parish leader and was very active there. It was in the evening so people were already gone—they had services in the morning. No one took responsibility for blowing the church up. The SADF accused SWAPO but SWAPO denied any involvement. To this day they don't know who blew the church up. It was a shock to everyone because they didn't know where the bomb was planted.

These events only strengthened the morale of the people. All of these South African atrocities were aimed at destroying the morale of the people but the people became more resistant. I remember a school in Okanimeikwa. Nobody knows who was responsible. It was during the night that the school was blown up. The South Africans set up a certain strategy to win the hearts and minds of the people—by blowing up schools and destroying the buildings—all this was blamed on SWAPO. The South Africans would say "OK you're helping SWAPO. Can you see now we ask you for information about them, can you see what they're like." It was propaganda to turn people away from SWAPO. If someone destroys your property, you're going to hate them. People become aware that all these things are being done to demoralize them.

---

[32] Ibid.

6. ACCOUNTABILITY FOR SOUTH AFRICAN ABUSES

Though Resolution 435 required both parties to the conflict to release all political prisoners, they were not obligated to provide information about those who had disappeared. In the summer of 1989, the South African security forces released a number of prisoners without disclosing what happened to those who had gone missing in their custody. The information that became available on disappearances resulted from legal proceedings filed by family members.

EXECUTIVE AMNESTIES

Over the years of armed conflict, security force personnel were charged and convicted of abuses in a few cases, though sentences were generally light, to the point of being derisory. For example, the two SWATF soldiers who burned and fatally injured the elderly Mr. Ndara Kapitango were fined a total of R50 (US$20).

Even more troubling was the practice of granting accused security force personnel amnesty. Former Koevoet members Leon Lotz and Pieter Bouwer were accused of murdering two civilians, survivors of the Kassinga massacre who had subsequently been detained at Mariental. After their release, they visited relatives in northern Namibia. One of the victims was Petrus Sankarie whose case is described above. It had been taken up by the law firm of Lorentz and Bone. An inquest determined that Lotz and Bouwer took the two into custody for interrogation, murdered them and buried the bodies in a water-filled pit. Lotz and Bouwer claimed that they had shot two terrorists and did not know that their victims were civilians. The Administrator General granted them amnesty because, he said, they acted "in the heat of the armed struggle." The amnesty was conditional on the two men leaving Namibia immediately.[1]

At times, South African State President P.W. Botha intervened personally to bar prosecution. In July 1986, he blocked the trial of the four South African soldiers charged with murdering Franz Uapota, whose death is described above, by invoking Section 103 of the South African Defence Act on the grounds that the soldiers had acted in "good faith."

In September 1987, murder charges were brought against the commander of SWATF's 101 Battalion, two colonels and three other officers in connection with the death of Immanuel Shifidi. A former political prisoner, Shifidi had been imprisoned on Robben Island for eighteen years. He was stabbed to death as some fifty armed men, dressed in civilian clothes, attacked a SWAPO rally in Katutura township on November 20, 1986. Wielding pangas (machetes), knobkieries (heavy wooden implements), bows and arrows, they charged a crowd of 3,000 gathered to mark the United Nations' International Year of Peace. Riot police in Casspirs fired teargas and rubber bullets at the crowd, including those fleeing the site.[2] The attackers were subsequently identified

---

[1] Mark Verbaan and David Lush, "Two Koevoet men are reprieved before justice runs its course," *The Namibian*, November 17, 1989, p. 1.

[2] Jean Sutherland, "Bow and arrow thugs wreck rally," *The Weekly Mail*, December 5–11, 1986.

as members of the 101 Battalion, an ethnically-based unit from the north, who had been brought in to disrupt the rally. State President Botha intervened and granted them immunity on the grounds that they were combatting terrorism.

Even in cases where inquests determined that a prisoner was murdered by the security forces no prosecutions were brought. In 1983, the Supreme Court of South West Africa ruled that Johannes Kakuva had been killed in detention and identified three officers allegedly responsible. No legal action was taken against them.

Although South African soldiers and police were shielded from prosecution for acts committed "in good faith" during operations, some soldiers, Koevoet members and other security personnel were prosecuted and jailed for abusing civilians in Ovamboland. Typically these involved the lowest-ranking personnel and concerned incidents where the military command could claim that the perpetrators acted far beyond the scope of official orders in torturing or murdering civilians. Two Koevoet members, Jonas Paulus and Paulus Mattheus, were accused of eleven counts of murder, rape, attempted murder and robbery after a night's rampage when, dressed in SWAPO uniforms, they terrorized civilians. Paulus was sentenced to death and executed; Mattheus was imprisoned for 12 years.[3]

APPOINTMENT OF OFFICERS FROM THE SOUTH AFRICAN COLONIAL REGIME

As Resolution 435 was implemented and independence approached, most of the SADF and the Koevoet commanders returned to South Africa while many members of SWATF, SWAPOL and Ovambo members of Koevoet remained in Namibia. When the SWAPO-led government took office in March 1990, it appointed some security officials of the colonial regime who had been linked with abuse to responsible positions in the security apparatus of the new government.

One of these was Colonel Gerrit Badenhorst, the officer in charge of interrogation for the Security Police. At the infamous Osire Camp, the interrogation of witnesses and the accused was conducted under his supervision. Badenhorst had responsibility for the beating of Erastus Uutoni. Beatings of detainees in security police custody occured under Badenhorst's direction.

In March 1992, Gerrit Badenhorst was one of several senior police officers suspended after a demonstration at which protesters were beaten by police using *sjamboks* (hippo-hide whips). Apparently, Badenhorst was not on the scene at the time. The decision to suspend him was made by the Cabinet. He was deemed to have acted unprofessionally and in neglect of duty. This suspension, however, does not substitute for the need to hold him to account for past abuses that he may have committed and that have been attributed to him.

---

[3] Cawthra, *Brutal Force*, p. 211.

The Namibian government has made similar appointments. Brigadier A.T.C. Nel had served in the Security Police since 1975 and while still a captain he had arrested Rauna Shimbode on April 15, 1977, in Windhoek. Shimbode was subsequently transported to the Security Police offices in Oshakati where she was tortured. (See above.)

Nel was also responsible for the infiltration of the law firm of Lorentz and Bone, the defense attorneys in the Swakopmund trial of Aaron Mushimba, by a Mrs. Ellis, who was hired by the firm in 1974 as a receptionist, clerk and telex operator. She had been a police informant since 1972. At Lorentz and Bone she opened the mail, had keys to the safe and access to files during office hours, and typed affidavits for four of the accused in *State v. Aaron Mushimba*.[4]

At her own suggestion she sought confidential and privileged information concerning the trial that she could pass on to Captain Nel from the typist for the attorney handling the case.

A partner in the firm, Anton Smit, was a friend of Captain Nel and admitted acting as an informant for him.[5] The firm demonstrated that confidential information on the accused had been extracted from their files and passed to the Security Police by these informers and the Supreme Court in Windhoek ruled that there had been "irregular and/or illegal departures from and infringements of legal formalities, rules and principles required for a fair trial which resulted in a failure of justice." Mr. Justice Hart said that the relationship between attorney and client had been "seriously breached."[6]

Nel was subsequently a senior officer of the Security Police under whose supervision and control detainees were assaulted.

Dereck Brune, who had been chief police spokesman in Ovamboland, was appointed to head security for the Independence celebrations. Brune is believed to have been a senior officer in South Africa's National Intelligence Service and was seconded to Namibia after a failed attempt to infiltrate the African National Congress in 1986. Before that, posing as a radical student, he was a police spy at Witwatersrand University and later testified against other student activists. His statements about events in Ovamboland had been denounced by SWAPO as "racist lies."[7] While Brune's stint overseeing security at the time of Independence was brief, he remains in Namibia's security forces.

Jacobus "Johan" Maritz, chief of National Intelligence continued as head of that Department in the SWAPO government. The Department of National Intelligence was established

---

[4] *State v. Aaron Mushimba*, 1977 (2) SA 829, 840.

[5] Ibid.

[6] *IDAF Focus*, September 1976.

[7] "Swapo's old foes reappear in top police posts," *The Independent*, April 28, 1989.

in 1987 to give the "Transitional Government of National Unity" its own intelligence gathering apparatus independent of the South African unit.[8]

These appointments were not publicly opposed in Namibia at the time. Later during the controversy over the appointment of Solomon Hawala, the government justified them by citing the need for national reconciliation and by referring to a constitutional provision, Article 141 ("Existing Appointments"), which states:

> (1) Subject to the provisions of this Constitution any person holding office under any law in force on the date of independence shall continue to hold such office unless and until he or she resigns or is retired, transferred or removed from office in accordance with the law.

The latter contention was without legal basis. As noted by the General Secretary of the Council of Churches in Namibia, Abisai Shejevali, "The Namibian constitution does not oblige the government to appoint persons who are allegedly notorious human rights violators . . . ."

There has been no known effort to investigate the abuses attributed to these officials.

---

[8] Ibid.

7. INTRODUCTION TO SWAPO ABUSES

After Angola won its independence from Portugal in 1975, SWAPO established a number of military bases in southern Angola. The organization's military headquarters was eventually located near the town of Lubango, 250 kilometers north of the Namibian border. Starting in the early 1980s, when growing numbers of SWAPO members and supporters were arrested by the organization's own security services as alleged South African spies, SWAPO established prison camps around these military bases. These facilities were expanded later in the decade to accommodate the ever-increasing number of such detainees.

The majority of detained SWAPO members interviewed by Africa Watch had fled Namibia after being involved from the mid-1970s to the early 1980s as high school students or workers in SWAPO-led protests against South African rule. After crossing the border into Zambia or Angola, often at great risk and difficulty, some were sent by SWAPO to study in Eastern European countries, Cuba, and Great Britain. Others had been with PLAN or in the SWAPO camps in Angola. A few were summoned from abroad by SWAPO leaders just prior to arrest, while others were arrested when they returned from abroad at the completion of their studies. Detainees were generally taken into custody by the SWAPO security services in the Luanda area and told that the Central Committee had ordered their transport to Lubango. There were no formal charges. In general, it appears that their unit or group commanders were involved in their arrests. Most of the former detainees interviewed by Africa Watch had heard by the time of their arrest that SWAPO was holding other detainees, but we did not learn of any significant attempts to resist arrest. Some were flown, others driven, to Lubango. Several of those Africa Watch interviewed understood that their long-standing membership in SWAPO did not put them beyond suspicion or arrest. They had believed, however, that they would be given an opportunity to demonstrate their innocence. Africa Watch's informants all denied spying or any other involvement with South African security forces.

The detainees were generally taken first to the Karl Marx Reception Center (KMRC) in Lubango, where they were initially interrogated and their luggage was thoroughly searched. Some were ordered to eat their toothpaste and ointments because it was rumored that the South Africans were sending agents with poison to kill SWAPO leaders. According to one ex-detainee:

> The Karl Marx Reception Center was originally known as the "screening board." It was the place where young people coming from Namibia were welcomed into SWAPO in exile and held for interrogation. Its name was later changed to the Karl Marx Reception Center.
>
> It was located close to a stockade for military discipline offenders, the Marxist Youth Center and the Onghulumbashe Base. The Defense Headquarters was about thirty kilometers away.
>
> The KMRC consisted of underground shelters that were used to house the guards and the officers involved in the interrogation. Another building housed the interrogation chambers. One was exclusively for interrogation; another for writing

confessions. There was another section with individual cells for people awaiting interrogation.

One officer there directed the tortures. The officers on duty rotated.

Another ex-SWAPO detainee interviewed by Africa Watch who asked to remain anonymous was born and raised near Gibeon in the south, joined SWAPO in the early 1970s and was educated in the south during a period of school boycotts and strikes that occurred in 1976. He left the country that year, taught in refugee camps in Angola and later worked in SWAPO offices in Luanda. He described his arrest when he returned from study in Eastern Europe:

When I arrived at the airport in Luanda from abroad in June 1984, I was picked up by security men and placed under house arrest. I was told that I was not to move out of the camp even though the usual procedure when one returned from a trip abroad was to report to his superior. When I asked whether there was some problem I was told by the camp commander that he had an order to keep me there. The camp was located on the outskirts of Luanda. I told him that I wanted to talk to the SWAPO representative in Luanda. There was no reason given to me by the camp commander. All I knew was that there was an order from higher up. I remained at the camp for five days when I was told that I had to go to Lubango in the south.

I was escorted by security to the airport at Luanda, was put on a plane and flown to Lubango. I was taken with three other people: one man and two women. The guy I knew from the time I had spent in Botswana. I knew one of the women by sight but did not know her name. The guy and I were taken in one covered truck at the Lubango airport and the two women were put in another similar truck. We were taken to a screening post that functioned as an interrogation post.

It was a pit in the ground which was covered by poles which were covered by leaves. From far off you couldn't see that it was there. The screening post [consisted of] three such pits which were not connected to each other.

The security guys at the screening post went through all my luggage, which they made me take with me from the camp outside Luanda. They went through the photos I had taken with me from the time I studied in Eastern Europe—pictures of friends I had made there. They tried to get me to say that these were South Africans, but there was an inscription on the back of the pictures written in the country's language. They took all my books. They made me taste all my toothpaste and even hair oil because there were rumors of poison. I had a radio with a transformer that came from Eastern Europe. They asked me about it. They opened it with a screwdriver, even though they thought it was a landmine.

Another ex-SWAPO detainee told of similar experiences. This man was born near Keetsmanshop in the south and did his secondary schooling there. He was active during the school strike in solidarity with the Soweto students in 1976 and left Namibia shortly thereafter to avoid arrest. He taught in a SWAPO camp in southern Angola and then was sent abroad on assignment by SWAPO. He described his arrest on his return to Angola in the summer of 1983:

When I arrived at the airport in Luanda, there were two cars waiting at the airport: one minibus and another small car. I was told to get into the small car. I was taken to a house which I later learned was the house of SWAPO security. I didn't suspect anything, everyone was very friendly. They asked me about my studies. Later I suspected that it was a plan to keep me busy. I had no problem answering their questions and sharing my experiences with the comrades.

On the same day, just before midnight, Philip Mavulu, who had collected me at the airport, kept coming in and out of the house. Finally he called me to his room and said that I had to report immediately to Lubango, the headquarters of our military efforts. After that he locked the door. At 6:00 A.M. two security guys took me to the airport and accompanied me onto a plane. They stayed with me the whole time. We arrived in Lubango near 8:00 A.M. There I was greeted by James Hawala, the SWAPO chief of counter-intelligence. James Hawala was later arrested on the charge of spying. He took me from the airport to what used to be known as the Karl Marx Reception Center. That was the place I was taken to for questioning.

We arrived at 12:00 noon and they gave me a room. They told me that under no circumstances was I to leave the room without notifying them. By then I felt that I was effectively under detention. I thought that there was something wrong. I was a member of SWAPO in good standing for a long time. I had heard about detentions and it came to my mind that perhaps someone had implicated me. I was aware that people had been arrested. Proportionately speaking, the ones from the south and center were the major targets. They had stopped calling me comrade and I put one and one together.

I was searched and my possessions were searched. They opened my personal letters, correspondence from friends were taken from me. No reason was given. I was told to eat the toothpaste that I had with me and put the vaseline ointment I had on my skin. At night I was locked up. Whenever I had to go to the toilet I had to knock on the door. The reason was that first someone had to monitor the situation, to make sure that no one saw me. I had to go under military guard to the toilet.

Yet another ex-detainee told Africa Watch:

One morning in late 1986, a certain political commissar of the Luanda transit camp called me to one side. He said he wanted my assistance to take care of a few things. He wanted help in a warehouse close to where the SWAPO military trucks were parked. It was part of the strategy that I was taken to that point. There was a padlock on the warehouse, and I was not suspecting anything funny or foul play. Then another chap came along. It was Mavulu's deputy, the deputy military attache in Luanda. He came up to us and started talking to the commissar. He said that he was under the instruction of the SWAPO Central Committee to see that I was taken to Lubango immediately. The political commissar acted surprised but I realized later that it was a set up. Finally he agreed and left me there with the deputy military attache and another chap who had a shot gun. This guy pointed his gun at me to move me along to the convoy of trucks lined up outside the warehouse. I said, "What's going on?" He said, "We are under instructions . . . we have to go to Lubango." By this time the existence of the detention camps and torture chambers was public knowledge, although no one talked about it within the movement. There was a hope that I was going for re-training. The other chap asked if I had anything in my pockets like pens, notebooks or money.

We arrived at Ngunza in Kwanza Sul province. I was locked up in a barracks. I was always escorted by someone with a gun.

LEGAL STANDARDS

SWAPO claimed that the detainees were spies. Assuming that characterization is correct, they were still entitled to certain protections. Though spies do not enjoy the protection afforded to civilians or prisoners-of-war under international humanitarian law, they are, nevertheless, entitled to certain rights under customary international law.

The minimum standards for the treatment of detainees set out in the Geneva Conventions applicable to either international or non-international conflict, must be afforded to all.

Common Article 3 of the Geneva Convention, which applies to non-international conflicts, requires that those who are not in combat or no longer in combat must be "treated humanely." It prohibits "violence to life and person, in particular murder of all kinds, mutilation, cruel treatment and torture," and requires that before any execution is carried out there must be a judgment by a regularly constituted court which affords the accused the judicial guarantees recognized as indispensable by civilized peoples. SWAPO's conduct must be assessed in light of these protections.

INTERROGATION AND TORTURE

At the Karl Marx Reception Center, the arrested SWAPO members were interrogated to extract confessions and were tortured until they did confess. The techniques used included: repeated beatings with freshly cut sticks and strips of automobile tires; beatings while prisoners were suspended from poles; simulated live burials; and other mock executions. Ex-detainees told Africa Watch that the interrogators from the SWAPO security service were not interested in the veracity or accuracy of the confession extracted under coercion. It appeared that they were quickly satisfied with highly improbable, even outlandish, accounts, the more elaborate the better. Several detainees said that their interrogators volunteered to write the confession for them.

Prior to their arrests, many detainees had heard rumors of detentions by SWAPO. Yet when they themselves were arrested, they believed that there would be an investigative process which would allow them to clear their names. There was none. Detainees were neither charged with specific acts of espionage, nor presented with evidence to sustain a claim that they spied for South Africa. They were asked to tell their life stories to their interrogators and when they made no mention of working for the South Africans, they were told they had left something out. Invariably, they were asked the same questions: Who recruited you? When were you recruited by the South Africans? What was your mission?

The interrogators also sought the names of other SWAPO members allegedly spying for South Africa. The interviews conducted by Africa Watch suggest that this was not motivated by a genuine concern to investigate or ascertain facts. Rather it was an effort to cast an ever wider net to implicate more people; in some instances, the interrogators seemed to have a specific quota of names the prisoner had to supply. More arrests were made on the basis of these confessions. Africa Watch interviewed a detainee who had been summoned back to Angola from a foreign country because his name had been given under torture by a young SWAPO recruit. Such confessions constituted virtually the sole "evidence" against the detainees.

Many former detainees interviewed by Africa Watch said they had confessed—despite the painful misgivings they had about falsely implicating themselves as South African agents—because otherwise they might be killed; if they survived, they might be able to clear their names.

According to one detainee held at the Karl Marx Reception Center:

That first day, in the afternoon, a security officer who worked directly under Solomon Hawala, Chief of SWAPO security, came by. His name was "Ndjafa." He asked me what was I doing here and why did I decide to work with the enemy. I asked which enemy am I working with? He said, take this pen and paper and write out when, where and how I was recruited by the enemy. I said

I have nothing to write because I never was recruited by the enemy. He said, "When I come back I want it written out."

The next day I was called to an office. There was another security officer there who said, "Tell me about yourself." So I told him my whole life story—but I didn't say anything about the details of how I came to Lubango. He asked me, "Why did they bring you here?" I said, "I don't know." He said, "You left something out. We knew you when you were in Namibia; our people were there. Tell me when and why you started working for the enemy." I said, "I never worked for the enemy. There's some plot somewhere, don't pull me into it."

Then he said, "Take off your clothes." He then told me to do 100 push-ups. When I got tired, he began to strike me with his military belt. "Will you talk now?" he asked. I said, "I have nothing to say."

Then he ordered me to get into a small military car that was parked outside the office. I was blindfolded. I could feel the bodies of several other people in the car. We drove off. There was no talk among us at that time—it wasn't allowed. When the car stopped, we were taken out one by one. I became hysterical because I thought I was going to be shot. I delivered my last speech. I said something about I was fighting for justice, not this kind of treatment, in a free Namibia. I was kicked in the ribs.

I was tied to a tree trunk and my blindfold was removed. Ngaweya, a subordinate of "Ndjafa," was there, plus a doctor. There were also several other men. There were a heap of sticks already cut. They started to interrogate me. I began to hear screaming from all sides, coming from the other people who had been in the car with me.

They asked me two questions: how was I recruited and what was I to do? I told them that I was to take photos of the camp and then write articles on how bad SWAPO was. I invented the name of a policeman who recruited me. Then the doctor took me through the bush not far to a prison camp and I was placed in a prison guard's hut. This was sometime in early July 1984.

At the prison camp I saw the camp commander and the officer who was the secretary of the camp. I thought that these two officers might understand. I told them that I had lied to the others about being an enemy agent. The commander kicked me in the ribs. "You're playing with us. You tell them one thing and then tell us something different." I was taken back to the hut.

The guard told me, "Talk or they will kill you. You are not the first person to come through here. If you don't talk, they will take you to another camp and then kill you."

The next day a junior commissar came by. He chained my hands behind my back. He called me "the guy who doesn't want to talk." Also with him was Commander "Don't Worry" Mupetami. He screamed at me, "Will you talk?" I said, "I have told the truth, I have nothing else to say." He started beating me and kicking me. He put his pistol to my forehead and asked, "Will you talk?" I said, "I have nothing to say." He hit me over the top of my head with the handle of the pistol—my head started to bleed. He told me that he would be back again the next morning.

This detainee was taken out the next morning and tied to a tree. Commander "Don't Worry" Mupetami beat him with a stick and a strip from an old tire. After this another guard took up the beating until he fainted. On regaining consciousness, he was beaten again. He told Africa Watch:

At one point the Commander told me, "If you don't want to talk I am going to break your leg." He took a log and hit me on the back of my leg but I was able to move my leg away quickly. He then took a tire and began beating me with that.

I thought to myself, let me give them what they want or they will kill me. So I said, "O.K. I'll write a statement." They gave me paper and a pen. I made something up—I wrote I was sent by that man and trained by someone else. I was recruited in Berseba in 1974. After a SWAPO meeting there I was taken into the bush and agreed to work with them. I used part of an incident that had really happened near Keetsmanshoop. I wrote that I was trained at a police station near Keetsmanshoop and that my main purpose was to write propaganda and take photographs.

Then they asked who I worked with. I said that I was the only one and then they began to beat me again so I made up some names.

Then they asked me what I knew about different people. "What do you know about this man? Is he an enemy agent?" And then if I did not answer they would start beating me again. I said, "He is an enemy agent" and made up a story for him. They started asking me about specific officials in Luanda, "Is he an enemy agent?" I said no and they beat me so I would say yes. They asked about the Secretary for Labor and the Secretary for Foreign Affairs. They asked me about people I knew in Luanda. If I mentioned a name that they didn't want to hear, they would say "remove that name." I wrote a lengthy statement, maybe eight full sheets of paper.

Then they asked me who did I recruit? I said, I didn't recruit anyone, I was just to do propaganda. "What kind of propaganda?" I said, "Propaganda that armed struggle won't work." They said that it was impossible that I didn't recruit anyone and they began beating me again. So I made up names.

Another ex-SWAPO detainee, Johan[1], interviewed by Africa Watch also described the abuse he endured at the Karl Marx Reception Center:

They called me to an office early in the morning. I found a panel of six men sitting there at a long raised table. They asked me to present to them my autobiography. After I did that, they asked me questions: if I was arrested by the South Africans before leaving Namibia. When I said I had been arrested in April 1976—because of my involvement in the student movement—they asked me to give the name of the man who arrested me. I gave it.

Then, after having done this they told me that I had forgotten something very important in my autobiography which I had to think about and mention. Having done some mental searching, I asked for a chance to go back to my room. I was asking myself what had I forgotten. After lunch I was called back to the office to review/re-read my autobiography. I told them what I knew of myself. At that stage they told me that I shouldn't play tricks with them. They said that they were not interested in listening to my lies and they pushed a paper at me and said answer the questions on the paper. These questions included: When were you recruited by the South Africans? By whom were you recruited? What was your mission? When were you expected to report back to the Boers? What is the reward that you were promised by the Boers? I found these questions very strange. I stated that I used to be a SWAPO activist in the struggle at home because of my fundamental differences with apartheid and its policies. Unless you are trying to make me give a false confession, I was never on the payroll of the South African regime, so I can't answer these questions.

The next day, in the course of Johan's interrogation, it became clear how he came to be arrested: he had been implicated by others under torture. When Johan was leaving Angola on assignment he had met two young recruits in the Luanda transit camp. One was from his home region and knew his family, so Johan spent some time talking with them. Eventually, Johan learned the whole story:

Later, when I was put in a dungeon, I met a friend who told me what had happened to these two guys. They had proceeded to Lubango under the pretext that they were to receive military training, but when they arrived in Lubango they

---

[1] A pseudonym; the former detainee requested that his real name not be used.

were arrested. This happened in March or April 1982. The practice was that everybody who came from the south and center was arrested. In 1979, the South Africans introduced compulsory military training, so that many young brothers left the country in order to avoid serving apartheid.

These guys were arrested and tortured and they confessed—that they had been recruited by the Boers to come and poison the SWAPO leadership. When they were asked where the poison was, they were tortured and they said the poison entered with me. Then they were asked was this done on the Boers' instructions and they answered affirmatively. Then they were asked a third question: Was I a South African police agent at home. After making denials they were tortured and they said yes, I was a uniformed policeman. I couldn't blame them, it was misfortune or fate that I had met them in Luanda and I have no feelings of revenge against them.

Johan admitted to his interrogators that he had met the two men in Luanda and that he encouraged the one whose family he knew to write a letter home. His interrogators told Johan he was lying; that they had obtained information from both men implicating him in a South African espionage scheme:

I denied all these things. I tried to use reason and logic with them. I pointed out that it was just by accident that I had met them in Luanda; that as a high school student in the south I left Namibia because of the struggle; and that there was not time for me to be trained by the South Africans. They rejected this out of hand. "You have to tell us the truth. If you don't tell us the truth we'll forget about you"—meaning that they would kill me. That's when the torture started. They told me to undress myself and they stripped me naked. They bound my hands behind my back and blindfolded me and put a pistol to my forehead and asked me to tell them the truth.

I remained silent. By then I was really puzzled. They had no concrete proof against me and they wanted me to make a false confession. Then they instructed me to lay down and they started to beat me with sticks. This was in the office at the Karl Marx Reception Center. Two of the officers who were in the room did the beating. It wasn't a very intense beating. When I screamed they stopped. They untied my hands, removed the blindfold and instructed me to sit down on a chair. One officer was in front of me and two were behind me. The one in front pulled my hair. When I bent forward he punched me and the other two pushed me forward. As a result of this continuous beating, I was hearing funny sounds. With threats they told me to leave the room and prepare to come back. The beating must have gone on for thirty minutes. They said, "If you are not going to tell us the truth tomorrow, this practice will continue."

The next morning, they woke me up early and put me in a land rover. They told me to lie down and then they threw a blanket over my face so that I would not know the direction I was being taken. At the river, they gave me a spade to dig a hole. Since the dirt was soft it was easy. I dug a hole that was big enough for me to fit into. After that they instructed me to lay down on my back in the hole I had dug. Then they asked me to confess along the lines of the questions that were on the piece of paper that they had handed me. There were three officers who had been on the panel. Ndjafa who was a commissar of the Karl Marx Reception Center and an ordinary security guard nicknamed "Devil." They repeated the questions: "Who was the Boer who had recruited me." When I failed to answer the questions to their satisfaction, they began to cover my body with sand starting first with my legs. I was being buried alive. By the time the sand was up to my neck I was unconscious but I think only my face was left uncovered. I only regained consciousness when I was back in my room.

Then and there I thought what can I do except confess or else I will lose my life. Perhaps one day I will be able to clear my name but now I will give them what they want. That night Ndjafa came to me and asked if I was ready to tell the truth. I said you can call me to the office tomorrow and I will tell you what you want to know. Then he slapped me in the face—he realized my sarcasm. He said, "Don't tell me what I want but what the truth is." I said, "I told you the truth when I arrived but you didn't believe it." He said, "You want us to take you back to the same place?" I said, "No, just call me to the office in the morning."

The next morning I agreed with what the two guys had said about me and that I was a South African enemy agent. It is quite mindboggling to do something against your conscience but when you're dealing with people who don't respect human rights, given the mentality of the interrogators, I had to incriminate myself. I hoped that someone would survive or that I would survive in the hope of getting to the truth.

Another former detainee told Africa Watch:

They just wanted you to confess to anything. They didn't care what you confessed to. In actual fact they weren't investigating any crimes, they were just trying to neutralize people.

Still another former SWAPO detainee interviewed by Africa Watch had been arrested in Luanda:

When I arrived at the interrogation center in Lubango—the torture chamber—I was told to get into one of these cells. They took my watch and my wedding ring. I was told that my name was given to them by the Central Committee of SWAPO and I was told to reveal myself to them. "Reveal myself for what?" I had written out my autobiography. They insisted that something very, very crucial was missing from my autobiography. I tried to remember, maybe I left something out. They told a junior guy to get some sticks. "This is what is going to make you talk." I said, "maybe you can help me out." "We want you to reveal yourself so you can return to Luanda." They started beating me. There were five of them. I know them all by name, they were security guys. I would say to them that I have written all that I can and I started screaming. They were beating me with my hands tied behind my back. There were poles on the floor. My legs were tied to two poles and my hands were tied to two other poles. They beat me for hours. I started bleeding and crying. When they got tired, they said after we come back you must tell your story.

After several weeks they decided to take me to Etale. By then I was very weak. The guys would come from the interrogation center to Etale. At Etale, there were guards but the torturers would come from the interrogation center. Etale was an intense torture center for people who refused to confess. I was kept in isolation there. I was almost mentally finished—partly because of the beatings, partly because of the psychological pressures. One morning I was so weak they said, "Go back to your cell so that you can be beaten up properly." I was so sick. The beatings continued. One of the medics at Etale Center developed a soft spot for me. He said to me, "Why don't you just say what they want? For your information, if you go on with this, these guys will kill you." "But what do I tell them?" I asked. "Just tell them any story. You can tell them any nonsense. They will even write it for you."

When I was very young I read comics, spy thrillers. I couldn't believe it.

Oswald[2] made up a story about his assignment. His confession demonstrates that credibility was not required:

One day when I went to the toilet I told the guard, "I want to write . . . just bring the paper."

This guy said to me, "Some of you are so stupid."

He didn't know how painful it was to say that you are a spy. I didn't know what to say. A guy came to my cell and asked me, "Are you finished?"

There was another chap, Charles. He now works at the SWAPO office. These guys get very nervous when you see them now, they turn away. He said, "Just write

---

[2] A pseudonym; the former detainee requested that his real name not be used.

your whole story: by who were you trained, how were you trained, when and where were you trained."

He gave me some broad ideas—I had some kind of structure. The next morning I was called to the torture center.

The guy said, "This is nonsense. You haven't written anything. Do you think we're stupid? What was your specific mission? For example, some of you were sent to kill President Sam Nujoma. Some were sent with tablets, some with guns."

I figured if I said I came to kill the SWAPO leadership that would be too dangerous. I went back to the cell. I figured out how to make up a story that I came to steal SWAPO documents and I made up any Boer sounding name to go along with it.

They asked me about the payment I received. I told them I was given 600 Rand. They asked, "What were you promised as a reward?" I told them a big house, a nice car and 3,000 Rand.

Then the guy asked me about the duration of my mission. I said, "It was depending on the circumstances. I would be filtering documents out about how SWAPO students were trained, where they were trained." I told them I was to discredit socialism, to convince students it was an evil that we could live without.

They asked me how many documents I had sent out. I told them that I had only sent out one because it was so difficult to get them.

They started asking me whether I knew this person and that person who was arrested before I was. There were other people whose names just appeared on a list. They asked me if I knew them as spies. They asked me what I knew about their enemy activities.

If you gave them some information, it saved you from receiving a severe beating. Sometimes they would give us a quota, telling us that we must give them sixteen names. When you gave them a name that they had on a list they would nod and smile. They would write it down and you would spare yourself a few strokes.

THE DUNGEONS

After the interrogations were completed, the detainees were transported from the Karl Marx Reception Center to a camp in the vicinity of Lubango: Etale, Hainyeko or Ominya. Because of the limited space at the KMRC, some prisoners who had not confessed were transferred to Etale, where they were interrogated until they incriminated themselves. Etale developed a reputation as the facility where "difficult" prisoners were housed. According to one ex-detainee:

> Etale was in a heavily wooded area making it hard to detect. It was almost surrounded by swamps, making it difficult to enter and impossible to escape. The guard cabins were positioned very strategically.

> The Karl Marx Reception Center could only handle so many people for a limited period of time. There were people at Etale who had refused to confess. Guards came from the KMRC to interrogate them there. These people were kept separate from the others at Etale.

This same detainee described the other camps:

> There was the camp near the Tobias Hainyeko Training Center. This Training Center was for new SWAPO/PLAN volunteers undergoing military training. The prison there started as a facility for [trainees with] disciplinary problems. To my knowledge, there were two camps at Hainyeko but later there was a third one. It was from this place that most guys were transferred before their release. There was Shombee's Base, named after its commander, Shombee. There was Omungakwiyu which was under Commander Bwana Nampoli.

Another former detainee described Shombee's Base:

> There were several dungeons together; two big ones. If more "work" had to be done on you, they would take you to a small dungeon to get you to make a further confession or if they wanted you to implicate someone else. In one pit, maybe two meters by three meters there were five of us at one point.

According to one ex-detainee, as the date for implementation of Resolution 435 and the release of prisoners approached, SWAPO was compelled to construct a prison building to house certain detainees. At "Ethiopia," a prison was constructed out of adobe bricks:

> Lastly there was "Ethiopia." Due to the pressure on SWAPO to be able to show prisoners, they started building a prison with bricks. This was not underground. It had some fourteen to sixteen separate rooms. Prisoners who had been the focus of international inquiry and concern, or those who had held leadership positions in SWAPO, were held there, like Fritz Spiegel, Eric Biwa, Ben Bois and later James Hawala.

Ominya was located at the old Hainyeko Base. This base had been attacked by the South Africans during the SADF's "Operation Askari" and the assault was cited as an example of the work of enemy agents within SWAPO.

Many prisoners were held in "dungeons." Also known as "dugouts," these were pits dug in the earth, roofed with poles, leaves, tarpaulins, sand, and sheet metal. Some had bricks extending up a few feet around their perimeters. The effect was to disguise their presence to any but those in the immediate area. A few of the camps had several sand dungeons close to each other. The prisoners were not allowed to communicate with those in nearby pits. They were guarded by SWAPO security force personnel who lived in nearby cabins.

In one corner of each dungeon, there was an opening through which a ladder was lowered, the only means of entry and exit. The dugouts were very secure—it was hard for inmates to get out. Construction was much easier than building a structure with bricks; they could be excavated cheaply and quickly to handle the growing numbers of detainees.

One ex-SWAPO detainee described a dungeon at Etale to Africa Watch:

The dungeon was a hole with high walls. The walls were ordinary sand. On the top they put sticks and sheet metal which was covered with sand. When you walked nearby you didn't realize it was a prison. At one corner there was an open space for a ladder. That's how we went in and out—by the ladder.

At Etale I was aware of two dungeons. There was another next to us but we were never allowed to pass by it. The maximum number in this particular dungeon where you couldn't sleep comfortably was 35. The opening used to be covered and the ventilation was very poor in the dugout.

Some dungeons held as many as 100 prisoners.

Another ex-detainee told Africa Watch:

At Etale I was taken to a place where there was a very large pit that was covered. It was called a 'dugout.' They brought a ladder and I was told to descend. On May 1, 1985, after an unusually heavy rainy season, the dugout walls collapsed and we were taken to a maximum security prison that had stone walls.

The dungeons at Etale were the worst conditions that I had in five years. They were just a hole in the ground with logs over the top, covered with corrugated sheets. The only ventilation was through the trap door in the corner and the door was closed at night. It was so hot down there, you would sweat through the whole night.[3]

---

[3] Africa Watch interview with former detainee, New York, June 1991.

Etale originally had three dungeons: two for men, one for women. The conditions were made worse by frequent overcrowding as there was a constant influx of new detainees. One ex-detainee who was held at Hainyeko told Africa Watch:

> There were between 70 and 90 in the dungeon. If two people stretched out, their feet would touch because it was very narrow. These dungeons had a few feet of brick above the surface and the walls were brick. The floor was rough cement. The roof was corrugated steel. The overcrowding meant we were sleeping too tightly together and with more people arriving there was a need to expand. We needed more space.

> In November 1985, some inmates moved out, me included, to a very big dungeon. This big one could hold—when inhumanely overcrowded—100 people. We had 98 in there. As more were arrested, more overcrowding occurred. I was there from November 1985 until May 18, 1988—2½ years.

CONDITIONS IN DUNGEONS

Disease was rampant in the dungeons and camps. Beri-beri, a disease of the peripheral nerves caused by a deficiency of vitamin B1, killed a number of detainees. It is characterized by pain and paralysis of the extremities and severe emaciation or swelling of the body. Scurvy, a disease marked by swollen and bleeding gums and livid spots on the skin due to a diet lacking in vitamin C, was also reported frequently. Malaria was also common. One ex-detainee described some of these:

> We had at first various health problems. There was a lot of coughing from the dust and we would get pimples all over our skin that would give off yellow pus.

There were no sanitary facilities inside the dungeons.   Detainees were taken outside to latrines twice a day. At other times, if they had to urinate or defecate, they used tin containers. The prisoners emptied the tins when they were taken to the latrines.

> There was a place in the dugout that we used for toilet purposes. We used yellow UNESCO containers that had carried food or else tins. We used the tins for urine; the others for defecation. There was a specific place where we kept these. When we went to the toilet [outside the dungeon] we took these with us and emptied them.

According to one former detainee, they were allowed out of the dungeons to use the latrines in groups of ten:

> The toilet was a hole in the ground with sticks over it and we would sit down on the sticks. If you had to do it at any other time there were tins in the dugout which were kept in a hole and then later emptied.

According to ex-detainees, food was mainly cornmeal and rice. One detainee told Africa Watch that the porridge and flour that they were given were dirty:

At the start we ate porridge. Water was rationed in four-liter plastic containers. Some in another dugout had the job of collecting food in pans and then bringing the pans over to the dugout, where they were passed down the ladder. Six to eight people would group around the pans and eat from one of them. When things were OK, we would eat twice a day.

Food was brought into the dungeons in big containers that once had been used for ammunition. The women detainees did the cooking. The food was brought half way by the women prisoners and then we carried it down into the dungeon. We passed the food down the ladders; one guy handed it to the next. We had our own internal administration. We would divide the food up among the detainees.

Detainees suffered from malnutrition. When it appeared that a large number were becoming ill, the diet was improved. One ex-detainee said that Solomon Hawala, chief of the intelligence and counter-intelligence service, did not want a large number of detainees to die; accordingly, when the guards thought people were becoming seriously ill they would bring vitamins and more nutritious food.

For long periods, the prisoners were kept inside all day except for the twice daily trips to the latrines. When there was work to be done, they would be allowed outside on work details: building cabins for the guards, collecting firewood for them, carrying water or making bricks for construction. This was the only permitted exercise or movement outside the dungeons. They would get outside every day only when there was a major construction project. Inside the dungeons, there was nothing to do to pass the time:

There was no light inside, which is why reading was so difficult. Further down it was very dark. We were not allowed to read magazines that would inform us of what was happening. We were given magazines from the Soviet Union and the socialist countries but these were already censored and outdated.

At one point, prisoners participated in the construction of the building at "Ethiopia":

The building of the prison was the only exercise we got. Some of us appreciated it because it was our only chance for exercise. Sometimes we would do jobs—build houses for the guards, building furniture or collecting firewood for the guards. The guards were told that we were enemy agents. We had no shoes, only undershirts, even in winter. That was very inhuman treatment itself. The lack of fresh air, the poor diet. You couldn't read a newspaper.

Another former detainee told Africa Watch:

Exercise was not allowed because they thought you would get fit and run away. People were regularly taken out and interrogated.

We had some books to read—mostly Marxist literature— and then every once in a while the guards would pass us magazines.

The prisoners devised ways of passing time.

We used to make cards and dominoes from pieces of wood. Some guys were so skilled they made chess pieces. Some guys would just sleep without end. During the day you had three minutes outside. During the day it was so dark in the dungeon. Sometimes they would keep the hole open. One needed extra resources to survive. Some collapsed, they couldn't take it. You would just sit there for 3½ years. Some guys were there for nine years. We had no radio, no newspapers, no pens. Sometimes they would throw in Soviet press books or copies of *The Combatant, Namibia Today*. One time a guy stole a magazine with a piece about the implementation of Resolution 435.

Medical care was at best primitive. SWAPO first aid personnel would come into the dungeons. According to ex-detainees, many were barely trained. No matter the ailment, prisoners were generally given the same medication. One ex-detainee reported:

If you needed medical treatment, a man came with a small box of medicine. You could have any ailment and he would give you the same medication. They were military medics with three months' training. Many of them couldn't read or write.

Detainees rarely saw a doctor. Those interviewed by Africa Watch who were taken to a doctor were believed to be seriously ill. One ex-detainee told Africa Watch about his sole visit to a hospital:

The ladder was lowered. They called my name. I was shivering. They told me to take off my shorts. I thought I was going to be beaten when I got out. Normally they would whisper but then they asked me, "What size trousers do you put on?" They gave me shoes and a shirt. They told me to lie down in the *waz* [a Soviet built automobile commonly used by SWAPO in southern Angola]. They were waiting for another sick person. They put a blanket over my head and told me not to talk. Then they brought the other guy in. The guy was breathing heavily but I had no idea who he was. We drove for about ten kilometers and then I was taken to a secret clinic. I thought I was going to be released. They told me to sleep and that they would see the next morning. They came back with a bucket with warm water and soap. They told me to wash myself properly. When I was done, I gave them the soap back and they told me to keep it. Someone came in with a tray with milk, porridge, and sugar. I saw the guys, the torturers and I started trembling. They said, "Just relax. Tell the Russian doctors what's wrong with you."

Other detainees told of being taken to clinics just prior to release in the spring of 1989.

PHYSICAL ABUSE

Though the ex-detainees interviewed by Africa Watch did not report systematic torture or beatings while held in the dungeons, they were physically abused during interrogations to incriminate others. At times, abuse followed a perceived insult:

In prison we were used to implicate others. Many times I was called in to give information, and we gave information under threat. Many of my fellow inmates were really tortured. Or alternatively, if they were not satisfied that you had given them all the information they wanted, they would torture you. If someone had given information through torture you would be called out and asked why didn't you give the information to the authorities and then you were beaten by the officers. This was the order of the day.

While in jail there were no executions; beatings would take place when the guards would insult detainees and then the detainees would insult the guards back. Or when they would tell the detainees that they had heard plans that they were planning to run away even though there were no such plans. They would beat us then.

One ex-detainee who was beaten by guards at Ominya told Africa Watch:

In September 1987, one of the guards insulted me. I replied to the insult. He threw a stone at my back. I came up out of the hole I was digging with the spade I was using and I hit him with it. The ladies [the women prisoners] were yelling, "No, no." The guard wanted to shoot me. When he aimed his gun at me, another guard pulled the magazine clip out. They beat me up with sticks that they had soaked in salt water. Such a stick makes a bad wound. Then they put me back into the dungeon where I remained until 1989.

DEATHS

Many deaths occurred as a result of malnutrition, disease and infection. When detainees appeared critically ill, they would be removed to a nearby cabin or hut to die and were buried by the guards.

According to one ex-detainee:

I remained in the same dungeon. Three people died in November 1983. Gerson Job from Windhoek was one of them. There was a general situation of malnutrition. There was a lack of fresh food. We were only given porridge and rice.

It was malnutrition and lack of proper air. Our bodies swelled up. When they were real sick, we carried them to a room on the surface. [Two of the deceased] Gideon and Eliphas were Ovambos from the north. Gideon had been arrested for diamond theft but he skipped bail and fled to Angola. SWAPO security said that was just a pretext the enemy uses to infiltrate spies into SWAPO. Kalampas died on March 10, 1984. In September 1984 old man Pius Amutenya died.

Another ex-detainee said:

I know a couple of guys who died. One was a very young guy who had just come from northern Namibia. He had malaria. By the time we carried him out he was dead. Another chap who died was from the Caprivi area. He had developed problems with his chest. It was so dusty in the dungeons. His name was Joseph Munyaza. He was a longtime broadcaster on SWAPO radio in Tanzania.

There was a specific small dungeon where they would take sick people so that they wouldn't die in front of us. The ones who didn't come back, you can assume they died. Between September 1987 and January 1988, 25 guys died. That's when the guards got completely frightened. They thought that we would all die. They took us to see Soviet doctors at a hospital. That was the only time we went to a hospital.

It was a secret clinic. I had no idea where I was being taken to. It was during the night. I thought I was going to die.

A friend of this former detainee related the circumstances of other deaths:

I saw more people dying between September 1987 and February 1988 because there was no food. That's partly why so many people died. We had beri-beri and scurvy. Lots of guys died of malnutrition. When people got sick there was no medicine, no drugs.

While there, problems with beri-beri came back. One man suffering from asthma died on the 15th or 16th of September. His name was "Stranger" Basson. The day after his death I was transferred to another dugout.

The detainees spent years in these conditions. Africa Watch interviewed detainees arrested in 1984 who spent five years in captivity. The conditions in the prison constructed by the detainees at "Ethiopia" were also bad.

TRANSFERS AND DISAPPEARANCES

Prisoners were transferred from one dungeon to another, or from one camp to another, without explanation. Many of those reported to have disappeared can be traced to a specific dungeon, but then disappeared on transfer. A former detainee described the arbitrary nature of the transfers:

In April 1986 people were selected from all the dungeons. I don't know what the criteria were. They just called out your name, date of birth, date of arrest.

While at Etale in April 1984, people were called out, I don't know why. In our analysis, they called out people who had just come from Namibia and people who were not well known in SWAPO. The transferees tended to be from the north or people who were not well known inside SWAPO. Not any of them I know has come back. Many of them are from my own tribal areas. When we met the families, they asked us [about their relatives]. They are still unaccounted for. The transfers took place from other places as well. From the intershuffling, we would meet new people. Our rough, conservative estimate was that between 130 and 140 people were transferred out. None of those from among my own tribal areas—including relatives and close friends—ever returned. Among those who I know never returned were Daniel Vreis, Edward Goliath and Joseph Fregiel Motinga. These were relatives of mine who were transferred in 1984. I had friends—Deol Boois, Capro Ngsapurue and Geoffrey Tjizera who were transferred out in April 1986 who have not returned.

In August 1986, people were gathered from two dugouts and were taken away. This left 30 people in my dugout. The people who were taken out were never seen again. One of them whose name I remember was Nicodemus Basson. He was from Berseba. He had formerly worked in the security service. Nothing was said about why or where they were taken.

One night in September 1985 we heard the sound of trucks behind the prison. We were told to take our belongings and we went to the trucks parked in the bush. There were two trucks. At first just one block [was transferred] but later the other guys joined us. At one point, neighbors from Etale who had been in the other cellblock moved in with us because there was overcrowding at the other prisons. They didn't want the newcomers mixing in with the vets—these people might have new information. They wanted to prevent that information from being exchanged.

WOMEN DETAINEES

A number of women were detained by SWAPO in the camps in southern Angola. They were used to perform such chores as cooking, making bricks and tending gardens. Africa Watch interviewed several who had left Namibia in 1981 by crossing into Botswana. They had been SWAPO activists before leaving Namibia. One of these women was later sent by SWAPO to Eastern Europe for further training. On returning to Angola, she went to work in the SWAPO transit camp in Luanda. Her account of her arrest resembles those of the male detainees:

In November 1984, I was told to pack my things. I was not told much else and I was told not to ask questions. I was prohibited from going to the administration. It took five days to reach Lubango. En route I met people who had been sent to Cuba whom I knew. I told them I don't believe that we'll be coming back. But I thought that there must be a procedure. I couldn't believe my friends were enemy agents. Most of the people from the southern region were labelled as spies. The only proof was confession obtained under torture and inhuman treatment. I arrived at Lubango on November 23, 1984, along with people coming from Cuba. We reached the so-called headquarters of the Secretary of Information of SWAPO—the screening center. The people who were suspected were to be screened there. The next morning I was told to select my luggage—I didn't take much because we knew what was happening if someone was commanded to go to Lubango.

Another woman told Africa Watch of her experiences:

In January 1984, I was called by my commanding officer. He told me I was being transferred but I knew something was going on. Andreis Basson, a colleague of mine, had disappeared. I was told to pack my things and go the next morning. I called my chief and asked whether he was aware of my transfer. He was not aware of it. I knew what was going on.

I was taken to a prison called "00" or Kilimanjaro. There people told me to take off my shoes. They said it was an order. I was taken very far away into the bush. I was told to undress while the interrogators stood there. I was put into a dugout.

The interrogation and abuse the women were subjected to were similar to that experienced by men:

A security man knocked on the door and said "Come." Sometimes they came with smiles like comrades. You started the interrogation, you would be asked several questions: When were you recruited, where were you recruited and who trained you. When they asked me why I came to this place I said because I was commanded to. Then they told you to undress. If you didn't, they would undress you. They did not have any respect. Sometimes they would leave you in your panties. They used sticks. It was very painful. They left terrible scars.

They asked you what you were doing before you left the country. During the process one of the torturers would give you a clue. One interrogator would say, "Just admit, you are not the only one. Even the leadership is involved." They would beat you until you were unconscious and then the first aid people would come. The next day they came back. They asked, "Did you not feel pain, see you have bloody scars."

Another woman recounted how she was coerced into falsely implicating a friend at the Karl Marx Reception Center:

They came to me one evening in May 1984. The security people called and said, "We are taking you now to someone whom you know very well. If we take you there you must go and tell the truth." I was not happy about this. They took me to the Karl Marx Reception Center. I was accompanied by so many guys with guns. When I came into the office I saw Ida[4] sitting there. We were sitting facing each other. So I was asked whether I knew this woman. I said, "Yes."

"How do you know her?"

"We were living in the same place in Katutura, near Windhoek."

"Do you know her in any other way?"

"We were trained together by the Boers."

Then I was taken away.

The main interrogators were David Ngaweya, Justus Kanandjembo, and Commissar "Ndjafa."

The woman who had been implicated in this manner told Africa Watch:

I resisted for five months and then I was taken to the jail. They would bring people to identify you. They used force to get them. If you didn't go along with it, then you'd be shot. That was the program—there was no way out.

---

[4] A pseudonym.

In the morning I was taken to Ominya base where the majority of the women were kept. It was one of the most notorious camps for the detainees. We called the Commander "Hitler." The guys called him "Don't Worry."

Detainees told Africa Watch of deaths among the women detainees. According to one ex-detainee:

One lady died. She had a pain in the stomach. She was groaning and was taken out. Her name was Sonia. I remember another woman, an elderly lady in her mid-50s, named Martha Angulla. She died on June 14, 1988. They carried her out on a stretcher. That was the end of her. If you did not come back after being carried, we knew that it meant the person had died.

Nevertheless, the women detainees resisted their mistreatment. Some went on strike on May 1, 1989. Those who joined in were beaten. One woman who participated in that strike told Africa Watch:

Later we decided we were tired and we stopped fetching water, except for cooking, and on May 1, 1988, we started our strike. It was spontaneous. We were beaten up that night. We were told to strip and that "your buttocks should face the roof and your legs should face Angola with your stomach on the ground and your head facing Namibia." They beat people trying to find out who organized the strike.

That night we were told that we wouldn't see the sun rise again and we were taken to the side where the men were held. Thirty-six women were not allowed outside after the beatings, we were under "house arrest." We were punished and released from "house arrest" on September 6, 1988. We couldn't see one another.

PREGNANCY AND CHILDBEARING IN THE DUNGEON

The women detainees had particular problems. One ex-detainee told Africa Watch:

We had no sanitary pads. No water to wash with during that period. Pregnant women suffered especially.

There was a woman who was pregnant. She gave birth in a dugout in the darkness. When they got pregnant they were kept in the dugout. This girl had labor pains. There were women who were qualified as midwives, nurses and doctors, but they were not allowed to practice anything because we were being punished. The woman was 7 months pregnant. Her name was Jacobina Kashima. She started bleeding. She used to report her troubles but they didn't care or take her to the doctor. This girl started bleeding and we started knocking. This lady went to the spot where we relieved ourselves. She screamed, "It's coming out."

A woman, Theresa Basson, who had studied medicine for four years came over. The umbilical cord was strangling the baby and he was born dead. Finally the guards brought an old razor blade and cut the umbilical cord. The women took off their tee shirts to wrap up the infant. The mother did not see the ground where her infant was buried.

Another woman, Karen Ofeeku, was apprehended while pregnant. She was beaten. The child she gave birth to didn't move. She was abnormal. She couldn't hold her neck up. When the child died that lady did not even see the grave of her child. There was no way of consoling her.

CHILDREN

Children were detained in the camps with their mothers but were kept separate from them and reportedly beaten by camp guards. The children were held in a room and locked in at night. According to one former detainee:

There were around 17 children at Ominya Base. My child was left in a day care center. He was beaten there. He ate dry fish. It was an unhealthy diet. The child was in day care run by the guards and then he was put in the cell with me.

When taken to the barracks I no longer had care of my children. I was classified as one of the stubborn ones. I was denied contact with my child. For one year, I was kept under house arrest for asking questions. In January 1987, "Hitler" was slapping my child on the face. On February 26, 1987, our children left. We were told by Solomon Hawala and the Minister of Defense that SWAPO decided to take our kids. The kids were innocent. It wasn't right to take our children. They said they were taking our kids to a kindergarten but when I was released I saw my child for the first time in two years. He was dirty. I took it for granted that they would go to the kindergarten but they took our kids and distributed them among Ovambo-speaking people. One girl, a beautiful child, was neglected by the woman taking care of her. She [the child] drank a bottle of Angolan home brew and she was paralyzed. My child was beaten daily.

8. THE RELEASE OF THE SWAPO DETAINEES

By early 1989, as the date for implementation of Resolution 435 drew near, SWAPO announced publicly that it was holding 201 "South African spies" and that they would be released according to the terms of the Resolution. On May 24, 1989, observers from the United Nations Transition Assistance Group (UNTAG) recorded the names of detainees released from custody near Lubango. Though SWAPO did release detainees, the procedure prevented an accurate accounting.

The detainees were required to swear loyalty to SWAPO as a condition of release; if they did not, they were told they would be handed over to their "South African masters." They were informed that they were being treated leniently and then threatened with death if they betrayed the party in the Constituent Assembly elections scheduled for November. Prior to release, they were ordered to make videotaped statements about their espionage activities. According to ex-detainees interviewed by Africa Watch, several prisoners who did not consent to repeat previous confessions were segregated from the others and have not been seen since. One former detainee told Africa Watch:

> As it got close to release time, in November and December 1988, a delegation arrived with videos [cameras] again. The delegation included only the military and security services and was headed by Solomon Hawala and another officer whose combat name was Bongi. What was new was that all of us without exception appeared before the video cameras to be interviewed. We were told not to change our statements. Some of us who they were unsure about were asked whether we would change our statement. Three guys—Gerhard Tjozongoro, Tshutheni Tshithigona and "Mandela"—said that they were going to change their statements. They said that they had lied enough, that they were tired of lying and whatever will happen, will happen. They were immediately taken away and beaten. One of them was kicked in the ribs by the guards. None of them have been seen to this day. Since we knew that the delegation was composed of members of security, most of us didn't change our statements.

> On January 10, 1989, we had a visit from Moses Garoeb [SWAPO's Administrative Secretary], who told us that a decision had been made to release us and that we would be going back to Namibia and we would be expected to campaign for SWAPO in the elections. Should we turn against the organization, we would forfeit the last chance we were being given. We were asked if we were ready to go back and campaign for SWAPO. At first I was quiet. At which point he said, "Well, I know that you are intelligent people so I would like you to think twice." He repeated the question. The way we understood it was that we were in a very dangerous situation. The second time, a small group said, "Yes." I never shouted so loud as at that time. It's now or never I thought. The third time everyone said, "Yes." Then they promised to release us.

Another ex-detainee told Africa Watch of visits by leading SWAPO officials in that period:

In March 1989, Garoeb came to Ethiopia Base with Hawala and the Secretary of Defense. Garoeb said: "Do you want the party to release you?" We said, "Yes." "Do you regret what you have done?" Everyone was quiet. Garoeb said, "You didn't understand what I am saying. If the party releases you, will you work for the party?" "Yes," we answered. "OK, SWAPO is prepared—in the spirit of forgiving but not forgetting—to let you go. If you get out and work against the party, there will no second pardon. There will be no mercy." He told us that we would be released soon.

In April, Hawala came back. He told us there was an agreement between SWAPO and the South Africans and that prisoners must be released but that SWAPO would only release us if we signed an oath on a piece of paper. It was issued by the SWAPO leadership. It said, "I pledge I will remain loyal to SWAPO. I won't engage in anti-SWAPO activities and will report such activities to the appropriate authorities."

At Ethiopia we were brought supplies: clothes, trousers, shirts, and tennis shoes. We got on trucks and were taken where there were structures. We slept there. They promised to bring a leader. They brought the Secretary of Defence.

On April 19, 1989, we were set free.

During this period, seriously ill detainees were taken to clinics and hospitals to regain their health before release. According to one ex-detainee, Solomon Hawala stated that they were "too ugly" to be released directly.

THE RELEASE OF THE 201—MAY 24, 1989

SWAPO attempted to choreograph the release of the 201 whose detention it had publicly acknowledged. Their release was scheduled to take place before a corps of foreign reporters brought by SWAPO to southern Angola to hear the confessions of those released and record their pledges to rejoin SWAPO. These detainees were well fed prior to release.

Just before the releases, Solomon Hawala appeared and restated the choice for the detainees: to swear loyalty to SWAPO or be handed over to the South Africans. Shortly thereafter, the assembled detainees were introduced to foreign journalists. UNTAG observers in Angola recorded their names, but with the journalists present, the detainees denied that they were spies and recounted their experiences in detention. Several removed clothing to reveal their scars to the journalists.

They told the foreign journalists that they were not prepared to stay with SWAPO; they wanted to send a message through the journalists that they were being coerced. The next day, security forces led by Solomon Hawala returned to the camp and destroyed the structures that had been used to house the detainees. Afraid for their lives, the prisoners fled into the bush. Eventually, they made contact with the ICRC and came under its protection. Of the 201 detainees, forty-eight decided to remain with SWAPO and were repatriated as SWAPO members. On July 4, 1989, the remaining 153 arrived in Windhoek aboard a UN transport plane.

One released detainee described the staged release to Africa Watch:

Toivo ja Toivo [now the Minister of Mines and Energy] came with a message, a resolution about reconciliation. SWAPO had decided to release and pardon us. They would bring UNTAG observers. They asked if we wanted to see foreign journalists. Toivo came with a delegation. The first day Toivo chanted, "Viva SWAPO." We all joined in. It was the only way out.

The next day he came with the foreign journalists and UNTAG. Toivo shouted, "Viva SWAPO." No one joined in. We wanted to tell our story and we did. We told of the choice we had been given: repeat our loyalty to SWAPO or be handed over to the South Africans. So we declared we would stay with SWAPO. We explained why we had acted in that way. People started showing scars to the journalists.

Toivo was surprised. He said to Garoeb, "Come over here." He said that he would go back to the Central Committee and explain the situation to them.

The UN was not prepared to take us. They said that they would inform the Angolan government and they left with Hawala.

Generally the UNTAG officials were not sympathetic. According to one ex-detainee:

The UNTAG officials were brought to witness our release. But we contradicted the leadership. We were labeled as spies but we wanted to tell the truth. We asked Colonel Moriarty from Ireland for assistance and protection. He said O.K. he would come every day but he never came back.

Another ex-detainee told Africa Watch:

Initially we were registered with SWAPO, which would have smuggled us into Namibia as ordinary refugees.[We refused this.] We told UNTAG that they couldn't just leave us there. They must leave soldiers to protect us. If we didn't make our own escape, I don't know what would have happened to us. Solomon Hawala and soldiers would have come back to do us harm.

Another among the 201 reported:

The next day, journalists came from Germany, France, Cuba, Namibia and the Soviet Union. We told our story. They had been told that we would confess and that we were prepared to integrate with SWAPO. We had been given two options: 1) rejoin SWAPO or 2) return to our "South African bosses." We rejected both options and took a principled stand.

This departure from the script provoked retribution. According to one ex-detainee:

The next day or the same day, Hawala returned with soldiers. Everyone ran into the bush. We were scared. They were going to kill us or re-arrest us, we thought. They started breaking down the structures they had built. They took our beds. They said, "You must get that from the UN, because you decided to go to the UN." We moved to beyond the river to wait for the UN.

Another former detainee told Africa Watch what happened next:

We fled into the bush and arranged to escape. Me and three others were delegated to go to Lubango, some forty kilometers away, to contact the International Committee of the Red Cross. A lady there took us to UNTAG and the Angolan government. With trucks, they gathered us. Many people were afraid and decided to stay with SWAPO. This left 153 of us. Forty-eight decided to stay with SWAPO. FAPLA [Angolan government's armed forces] troops came in force—there was a danger of their being shot at. We were taken to a camp under the care of the Angolans and the UNHCR [United Nations High Commission for Refugees].

We returned to Windhoek on July 4, 1989.

This method of release prevented an orderly accounting of the detainees held in the camps. SWAPO never released a full list of those it had detained.

Another group of ex-SWAPO detainees returned to Namibia on August 8, 1989. Not included among the "201," they made up another group of eighty-four detainees who began to fear for their safety when they had been left out. Sixteen broke off from the larger group and escaped to the custody of the UNHCR. Africa Watch interviewed one of that group about his experiences:

We were released on May 17, 1989. They took us into the bush to an old SWAPO training base. When released, we were eighty-four. We stayed there during May, June and July. We got a radio and heard that SWAPO only had detained 201 detainees. We realized that our number of 84 wasn't included in that and we thought that SWAPO was going to do something to us. So from there myself and one other fellow ran away to go to the UNHCR in Lubango. We went to give the UNHCR the list of the whole 84. We told them that we are Namibians who have not been returned. We want to stay in Lubango under UNHCR care. We don't want to be returned. We made a group of sixteen out of eighty-four. We took ourselves out from the group. The others weren't repatriated as ex-detainees. The sixteen of us were loaded on a cargo plane and we arrived in Windhoek on August 8, 1989.

The other sixty-eight were repatriated as Namibian refugees.

According to testimony obtained by Africa Watch, other detainees voluntarily agreed to remain with SWAPO and were repatriated as SWAPO members or Namibian refugees. One man who was repatriated to Namibia as a SWAPO member reported:

The actual release date was April 19, 1989. The Commander and the guards arrived. People were called out, searched and undressed. We were given new prison clothes and asked to get into the trucks.

On April 21, 1989, all our old things were burned—everything. I was transferred to a bush clinic at Ominya. This was also a SWAPO prison where the female prisoners were held. Since we were going to be released we had to be healthy—we were given vitamins and healthy food for an effective recovery.

On May 21, Andimba Toivo ja Toivo and Solomon Hawala visited us and we were supposed to confess. We were told that the SWAPO Central Committee decided to release us, but we had to state if we wanted to be handed over to our masters, the South Africans, or repent and go where SWAPO members were. We stated our desire was to be with SWAPO and we were not South African agents.

They asked me if I wanted to join my colleagues who had deserted, or SWAPO. I said, No, I wanted to remain with SWAPO. I was taken to SWAPO's "Lenin" base, where Solomon Hawala had a house. I remained there until I was repatriated under the UN Plan as a SWAPO member on July 29, 1989, when I was released as a free man.

A woman told of the circumstances of her release:

Our release happened suddenly. We were just called and told to queue up, on May 12, 1989. We were taken into the bush and met Solomon Hawala. We were told to take an oath that from now on we would be loyal to SWAPO. As we were reading that paper we were videoed. After reading the paper we were given a flower and taken to a settlement and given second hand clothing. We were not allowed to take anything with us. We were released with SWAPO. We were taken to another place and put into prefabricated buildings to sleep. They slaughtered cattle for us. Two weeks time went by.

Several ex-SWAPO detainees interviewed by Africa Watch stressed that prisoners who had been held with them were not released and have not been seen since. One ex-detainee affiliated with the Political Consultative Committee (an organization of former SWAPO detainees formed in Angola) reported:

> At the time of our release, we pointed out to several top officials of the Angolan government: the rest of the people are here, go find them. The Angolan government did nothing to search. At that time, approximately June 1, 1989, it was still possible to find people. We had names and locations. We put the blame on the MPLA [the ruling party of Angola] and UNTAG. UNTAG had a bias in favor of SWAPO.

> We have a list of those people who were jailed with us but who didn't return. There is a list of 590 people whose names we have gathered.

> Sometimes in the camps you would be transferred. That's how we learned of the number of people. Sometimes bribery was used to get information. It was difficult to give the exact numbers. A number of people we know from our area are missing.

> The Political Consultative Committee submitted 500 names excluding those who had been released. We gave the names only of people we knew or whom we knew the place where they were held. We did not give their military names. We knew scores of other people but we decided to be very conservative in our estimates. While still in exile, we gave people paper to jot down the names and places of where people were held. We emphasized caution and conservatism.

It is clear that many more than 201 detainees were held by SWAPO and that the organization deliberately frustrated any accurate count of those in its custody. Some who survived trickled back into Namibia, but the opportunity for a full accounting was lost. Today, some humanitarian relief organizations and ex-detainees believe that other prisoners who have not returned to Namibia are still being held somewhere by SWAPO, possibly in Angola.

Africa Watch was not able to travel to Angola or interview anyone who had detailed, credible information on this issue. Thus, on the basis of its research, Africa Watch cannot comment on these claims. There are, however, hundreds of Namibians who were last seen in SWAPO's custody whose fate is unknown. Only a full and open accounting by SWAPO can resolve this disturbing question.

9. THE UNITED NATIONS MISSION ON DETAINEES

During the summer of 1989, after the return of the former detainees to Windhoek, concern about past SWAPO abuses mounted. Several organizations which had been active on the detainees pressed their concerns. The Parents' Committee (PC), which emerged in the mid-1980s, had at first campaigned quietly for information on the fate of relatives who went missing in SWAPO custody. The PC had become very vocal about SWAPO's policies and was opposed to SWAPO politically.

In May 1989, the Parents' Committee brought a court action to secure the release of six people it alleged SWAPO was holding in detention in Angola. The Supreme Court in Windhoek ruled in November 1989 that five had been held up until May 1989 but there was insufficient evidence to rule that a sixth had been detained. The court said that it lacked the authority to order the release of prisoners held in Angola. It instructed SWAPO to account for the five, if they had been released after May.[1]

In September 1989, the Parents' Committee filed an urgent application in the Supreme Court in Windhoek against Sam Nujoma and six others. The application sought an order requiring the respondents to provide a list of those detained by SWAPO; the delivery of the records of detainees held at camps in Angola; and the release of a number of detainees. This coincided with the return of the United Nations Mission on Detainees.[2]

The Political Consultative Committee (PCC) was formed in Angola as a pressure group by ex-SWAPO detainees shortly before their repatriation to Namibia. Its agenda included efforts to campaign for the release of other detainees still being held, to publicize the abuses committed by SWAPO and to prevent SWAPO from coming to power in the UN supervised elections. At one point the PCC announced that it would not ally itself with any political party.

The PC and the PCC held dramatic press conferences in Windhoek where a number of detainees stripped to display the physical scars of their imprisonment. They estimated that much larger numbers were still being held by SWAPO. The issue of SWAPO detainees became a highly charged political issue.

In response, the Special Representative of the United Nations Secretary-General (SRSG), Mr. Martti Athisaari, dispatched an UNTAG mission—the United Nations Mission on Detainees (UNMD)—to visit SWAPO camps in Angola and Zambia. The Mission's main purpose was to determine whether any Namibians were still held by SWAPO at locations identified as "detention facilities." If there were any found, the Mission was empowered to make arrangements to return them to Namibia to participate in the election. The terms of reference also mandated that the

---

[1] Amnesty International, *Namibia: The Human Rights Situation at Independence*, AI Index AFR 42/04/92, p. 13.

[2] Southern Africa Project, "This Week in Namibia," September 17–24, 1989, p. 4.

Mission "determine the present whereabouts of the persons . . . alleged by various sources to be still in SWAPO detention in Angola and Zambia."

The Mission was led by Ambassador B.A. Clark, a Nigerian diplomat who was the UNTAG representative in Angola and included: officials from the Office of the Special Representative of the Secretary-General; UNTAG Police Monitors; Colonel Michael Moriarty, Chief Liaison Officer of UNTAG in Angola; and others. According to the Mission's final report, when the Settlement Plan was implemented, several lists of individuals allegedly detained by SWAPO had been received by Mr. Athisaari's office. After the release of the 201 on May 24, 1989, and the return of 153 to Windhoek on July 4, 1989, additional lists were received by the SRSG's office. Following the arrival of the second group of sixteen former SWAPO detainees in Windhoek on August 9, 1989, additional lists came in. In all, the Mission had compiled a list of persons, including those released or repatriated and those who reportedly had died in detention, of some 1,110 names. These included names forwarded by the Parents' Committee and the Political Consultative Committee. A list of alleged detention sites was also prepared on the basis of the information provided by the ICRC, the PC and the PCC. The UNMD made efforts to determine the fate of those on the lists.

The United Nations Mission on Detainees took place between September 2–21, 1989, and on September 6 the Mission visited several locations in Angola, including the Etale Camp, Ominya Camp, Ethiopia Camp, Shoombe's Base, old Hainyeko Camp, the Screening Center and others.

In Annex III, "Description of Locations Visited by The Mission in Angola and Zambia," the Mission described some of these facilities. Ominya Camp was depicted as "buildings above and below the surface level which had accommodation apparently used for the holding of detainees and for storage and classrooms." The camp appeared totally abandoned and most buildings had been stripped. Ethiopia Camp was described as a "well-constructed concrete structure set in a sheltered ravine and hidden by natural foliage cover. The buildings were about 3.5 meters above ground rather than sunken," and "had a dual corridor which was divided by a concrete wall and barred windows in each cell approximately three meters from the ground." This too appeared to be abandoned and stripped. The Mission described the Karl Marx Reception Center (the Screening Center) as a site "used for identification and registration purposes. There were sunken offices, storage facilities, accommodation buildings and several containers." Etale Camp, the site of the worst dungeons where detainees said they were held if they did not confess during interrogation at the Karl Marx Reception Center, was described as similar in design to Ethiopia Camp but the "cells were partly sunken into the ground." It had the usual cluster of administration, residential and storage buildings. The report stated that the Mission found that the "geographical locations as well as the physical layouts of the sites visited corresponded in the main with the original information."

The Mission visited a refugee settlement outside Luanda and a vocational center in Kwanza Sul. After leaving Angola the group proceeded to camps in Zambia.

On October 11, 1989, a formal report of findings was issued stating that virtually all the camps/sites in the vicinity of Lubango had been stripped of "all valuable material, e.g. beams poles, roofs, doors, etc." This indicated to the Mission that all the camps had been closed and abandoned several weeks previously and "[t]here was no evidence that any persons were being held against their will at any of these locations." Nor did the Mission see any evidence "that any person allegedly detained had been transferred from one of these locations to another area before the Mission's arrival."

The Mission also met and talked with Namibians it found in various settlements to determine whether they were there voluntarily.

The Mission concluded that "the majority of persons allegedly detained or missing have been repatriated or accounted for." Three hundred and fifteen were listed as being unaccounted for. The report went on to state that the Mission had "sought to obtain the fullest possible information from SWAPO." The response of SWAPO officials was, in general terms, that they were untrue and that all the detainees SWAPO held had been released." In Lubango, SWAPO officials apparently produced lists of those who had been released and repatriated that "corresponded almost entirely with the lists relating to the group recorded by UNTAG observers in May 1989 and the group of 84 detainees whose release came to light in August 1989." The report stated that those who had elected to remain with SWAPO had been repatriated under the ordinary repatriation program.

SPECIFIC FINDINGS

The report found that at least 914 individuals had been imprisoned by SWAPO. It separated the names into five categories: 484 released and/or repatriated; seventy-one not detained; 115 reported dead; fifty-two who could not be identified due to insufficient information; and 315 whose present status was unknown and required further investigation. The Mission issued a detailed, name-by-name breakdown of its findings in a series of Annexes to the Report.

Former SWAPO detainees interviewed by Africa Watch were highly critical of the specific accounting in the various Annexes. Several associated with the Political Consultative Committee pointed to inaccuracies and inconsistencies in the various Annexes. Annex V(a) listed those the UN Mission had determined were "Released and Repatriated to Namibia," numbering them from one to 431. Annex V (b) listed those the Mission had determined were released and repatriated to Namibia because their names had appeared on a voters' lists for the November 1989 Constituent Assembly election. This Annex had fifty-two names, numbered 432 to 484. According to one former detainee affiliated with the PCC:

> UNTAG said that many people on the list were in the country. We know some of these people died. William Rukero [number 444] was found on the voters' list but he died. Joel Gariseb [listed as number 437] was with us all the time but he never returned. We have close ties with the families of these people. UNTAG claims that

numbers 432–484 were found on the voters' list, leaving only 315 unaccounted for. This is most outrageous.

According to former detainees interviewed by Africa Watch, the count of those in detention was distorted in another way. Annex VI listed "Persons Reportedly Not in Detention," with sixty-two names. This was suspect because several of those on that list were seen in detention. Africa Watch interviewed a former detainee whose name appeared in this Annex who said that he had indeed been detained. Another former detainee affiliated with the PCC went through Annex VI identifying those whom he knew were in detention:

Paul Daniel Casiano [number four] was a Namibian Angolan from Porto Alexandria who was with us. Shortly before we were released he was removed. The UNTAG mission claims that he was never detained.

Bience Gawanas [number ten] was a law student in London who was detained yet UNTAG said that she was never arrested.

Ismael Goagoseb [number eleven] is listed as working with the Council of Churches of Namibia. There is an Ismael Goagoseb who works for the CCN but there was another fellow by that same name who was with us.

Gerson Guiriab [number thirteen] is the nephew of the Foreign Minister. He died in March 1989 in front of us. He had malaria.

Aaron Mushimba [number thirty-five]. He was arrested in March 1989/4. He was tortured.

Sam Kavnawe Isaaks [number twenty-one] was held in the same prison with us but he never came back.

Peter Nanyemba [number forty], not the one who was the SWAPO Secretary of Defense. He was in prison with us. But he was put on the list.

Patrick Negumbo [number forty-one] was a top SWAPO official detained in 1986–87.

The Ngapurue brothers [Immanuel, Maleagi and Usiel, numbers forty-three through forty-five]. They were all in prison with us. None of them came back. UNTAG says they are living freely in Luanda.

Frans Woller [number sixty-eight] he fled in 1989 from SWAPO camps in Zambia and fled across Caprivi. He was captured by the SADF and tortured.

The Mission's report acknowledged that where similar names appeared on different lists it was frequently impossible to determine whether they related to the same individual or not. It stated that in the absence of information to the contrary, it was assumed when a name or a similar name appeared on two different lists, it referred to the same person. The testimonies obtained by Africa Watch raise concerns about the accuracy of this method of accounting.

LACK OF INDEPENDENCE

The UNMD did not take any of the former detainees on its trip to southern Angola and Zambia. In Annex III, of the Report, "Description of Locations Visited," the Mission states, "During the following six days contact was established with the local civilian and military authorities of the Government of Angola, including the General Officer Commanding the Southern Region, as well as the leadership of SWAPO." Former SWAPO detainees criticized the Mission to Africa Watch for its reliance on SWAPO and its failure to consult former detainees appropriately. According to one former detainee:

> To understand the UN Mission to inspect the camps, you have to look at the role of the UN in the whole transition process. Many people had raised the question of the SWAPO detainees. SWAPO and the South Africans had both agreed to release all political prisoners. The UN felt that if it didn't investigate, it would be discredited in terms of the implementation of Resolution 435 . . . it would fail. But the UN didn't do a thorough job. It relied on SWAPO and the Angolan government. They were depending just on them—the UN Mission assumed that everything would be put at their disposal and they didn't grasp the limitations that they would be operating under. So they wouldn't get at the facts or at least not in a genuine way.

Another former detainee associated with the Political Consultative Committee charged:

> The UN Mission came back with information and they had to work it out with SWAPO in terms of how to present it. They had links with people in the movement [SWAPO]. Clark came back, he knew certain things and he had to consult with SWAPO. That was the nature of the Mission and some of us knew that it was going to be a whitewash.

This former detainee went on to say:

> The UN Mission refused to take any detainees along on the trip to the camps. They said they didn't want any detainees.

Apparently sensitive to this charge, Mr. Athisaari responded in his statement issuing the Mission's report:

I have been asked why I did not include ex-detainees in the mission. The answer is simple. As a practical matter, I had obtained all the information needed to launch the mission as a result of extensive interviews with ex-detainees, as well as contacts with other sources, including the Parents Committee. By the time my staff had computerized all the relevant information received over many months from a whole variety of sources, I was in the possession of the most comprehensive set of data on the subject in existence anywhere.

But more important, as a matter of principle, the responsibility for seeing that all Namibians outside the territory are free to return home peacefully is, under the Settlement Plan, that of the Special Representative of the Secretary-General. That responsibility is shared with no-one else and will be carried out as called for in the relevant resolutions of the United Security Council.

However, relying exclusively on the assistance of the organization whose practices it was investigating while the Mission was in the field could have undercut its fact-finding ability. It certainly diminished its credibility among former SWAPO detainees and others.

In any event, the Mission was not mandated to, and certainly did not, establish accountability for the abuses committed by SWAPO in southern Angola; this task remains.

10. RESPONSIBILITY FOR SWAPO ABUSES

The first official SWAPO statement concerning the detainees was issued at a press conference in London in February 1986, in response to increasing international concern. SWAPO officials acknowledged that they were holding approximately 100 alleged South African spies. According to the organization's spokesman, the spy network, which was first discovered in December 1983, had penetrated both the political and military wings of the movement. Distinguishing between those who had been misled and the "real traitors," Mr. Theo-Ben Gurirab, SWAPO's Secretary for Foreign Affairs, said:

> SWAPO is not a charity organization but is engaged in the liberation of our country. These men have provided information to our enemy that was used for killing our people.

He said that the detainees would not be brought to trial and he acknowledged that human rights concerns had been expressed on their behalf:

> Concerns have been expressed about their well-being, where are these people, the conditions under which they are detained and the care which is given to them, whether they will have an opportunity to be heard, to have a right of appeal to the SWAPO leadership?[1]

While recognizing that there was a need for such information, he argued that:

> SWAPO is in a war situation and we are not able to open SWAPO up for scrutiny.[2]

At the press conference, SWAPO showed videotapes in which those interviewed described their activities on behalf of the South Africans.[3] Mr. Gurirab acknowledged that SWAPO was revealing the information because rumors had been circulating that SWAPO was engaged in "fascist" activities against Namibian refugees.

According to SWAPO Secretary of Information, Mr. Hidipo Hamutenya, who also spoke at the press conference:

> There is a well-calculated campaign organized by South Africa saying that SWAPO camps are concentration camps. We have apprehended some of these agents but

---

[1] "SWAPO alleges a massive spy network in its ranks," *The Namibian*, February 21, 1986, p. 3.

[2] Ibid.

[3] SWAPO had previously shown "confessions" made by detainees and videotaped by the SWAPO security forces. This was done to defuse concerns among SWAPO supporters internationally about the mistreatment of detainees.

we have not reached a step where we have become fascists against our own people. We have been, and will remain committed to basic human rights.[4]

By early 1989, SWAPO announced that it was holding 201 South African spies and that they would be released pursuant to Resolution 435. However, as discussed above, the release was flawed in several respects and SWAPO never provided a detailed accounting of those it had detained and released or of those who had died in custody.

At a press conference in Windhoek on August 23, 1989, Mr. Gurirab announced that SWAPO had released those it had held on charges of espionage. He called on anyone who believed otherwise to invite the ICRC, the UNHCR, and Amnesty International to identify and visit camps in Angola and Zambia where detainees had been held. SWAPO was still convinced that some of those detained had been hard core spies, he said, though he acknowledged that others could have been innocent.

With the releases, it became known that some SWAPO interrogators had acted brutally towards prisoners. This was regrettable, Mr. Gurirab said. He acknowledged that:

Some were tortured and that some of the officers charged with gathering information . . . had taken the law into their own hands and have carried out brutalities against these persons which we very much regret.[5]

Mr. Gurirab stated that such interrogators found in the SWAPO structure would be held responsible for their actions, a promise the government has failed to honor. Mr. Gurirab added that if the matter was not dealt with properly, the wounds of the war would never heal.[6]

The camps and dungeons were supervised by Solomon Hawala, chief of SWAPO security. The Karl Marx Reception Center and several of the camps were run by security service members responsible to Hawala. Former detainees interviewed by Africa Watch have identified specific individuals with varying levels of responsibility for abuses: the commissar of the Karl Marx Reception Center, the commanders of certain prison camps and individual guards. Though Africa Watch does not know the precise lines of authority under which the camps were run, it is clear that there was a chain of command at the Karl Marx Reception Center, where many of the beatings and abuse took place. The leadership acknowledged the existence of the camps publicly in 1986.

---

[4] Ibid.

[5] Cassandra Moodley, "Nujoma's wife was in Swapo jail, says ex-detainee," *The Weekly Mail*, August 25–August 31, 1989, p. 1.

[6] "We Detain Nobody," *The Namibian*, August 24, 1989.

The senior leaders of the organization were aware of these facilities. According to testimony taken by Africa Watch, several senior SWAPO leaders visited the camps and saw the conditions. Former detainees told Africa Watch that they tried to present information about their cases and treatment during such visits.

According to one ex-detainee held for six years in southern Angola at Etale and Hainyeko:

> We received visits of high level officials. The first high level delegation was made by Solomon Hawala, who was in charge of the prison and security services in November 1983. Hawala was accompanied by the chief of the President's security.

> The second visit occurred on November 1, 1984. At that time we said something on our behalf. "There is no denying that the South Africans would send enemy agents into SWAPO because they represent forces fighting for opposite reasons, but we feel that SWAPO should look at this soberly while in exile, because if you go back to Namibia without solving this, it will only discredit SWAPO and the Namibian people and only the enemy will benefit." It was an appeal to the SWAPO leadership.

> The response was very negative. "We could have killed you but, we don't want the world to make noise about it."

Several former detainees told Africa Watch of a visit by the SWAPO leader, Sam Nujoma. According to a woman who had been an active SWAPO member and was arrested in 1984:

> May 1986 was the first visit of Sam Nujoma. The second visit of Sam Nujoma was in April 1988. Every time he came we would tell him the procedure, the scars. He was still on the side of "his sons." He was believing them. Why don't you investigate the cases, we said. He said, "You were sent by the Boers and you will stay there until the time that we liberate Namibia and we take you to your parents. We will take you to Freedom Square and you will be judged by the people of Namibia."

Another former detainee, arrested in June 1984 after returning from abroad who had been held in Etale and then moved to Hainyeko, told Africa Watch of a visit by Sam Nujoma to Hainyeko:

> In April 1987 we had a first visit with the President. Our dugout was the lucky one so to speak because we always looked forward to seeing someone different so we could put our case across. We were paraded in front of the dugout. The President arrived accompanied by the Secretary of Defence [now the Minister of Defence], Solomon Hawala, and the presidential bodyguards. All the prison

guards were there plus reinforcements. Nujoma said, "Some of you chose to work together with the enemy and you will stay here until the independence of Namibia, at which point you are going to be rehabilitated."

He was nervous, he played with his foot in the dirt and he evaded my gaze. He was meek standing before the people when he called us enemy agents. At the end of his speech when he was about to go, some of us raised our hands in order to say something. The Secretary of Defence said that the President was late but the President half turned to answer the questions, you could see he was ambivalent. That he used the words "some of you chose . . . " meant that some of us could be innocent. The delegation then left.

Those who raised our hands wanted to pour out our frustration about being called enemy agents but I realized that it wouldn't help much.

Africa Watch obtained testimony from a former detainee about an earlier visit by President Nujoma to the camp where the female detainees were held:

On April 17, 1986, three of us from our dugout were prepared for a visit by the President. We were asked what were we going to say—they did that to "refresh" our memory and they told us not to change our story.

On April 21, 1986, he made a visit. He didn't see us; he just went to see the ladies who were being held there. He spoke to the ladies. After his speech the ladies became emotional—they were crying and shouting that they had been tortured. One lady whose name is Therese Basson who had been held for four years wanted to explain to the President how everything takes place. Solomon Hawala said, "Don't listen to that one. She's educated." Meaning either you won't be able to understand her or else that she would lie. Hawala cut the meeting short.

We knew all this because young boys and old men worked outside—the men cooked and the boys did gardening. One guy was caught going to visit the ladies and as a punishment they put him in with us. He was not there himself but he learned this from the ladies.

Still another ex-detainee interviewed by Africa Watch told of presidential visits to the dungeons at Hainyeko:

The third visit was in March or April 1986. The President himself visited us at Hainyeko. Initially we were asked if we were ready to see the leadership. He said, "I am addressing you in the name of Namibia's heros, the people you have betrayed. SWAPO of course is ready to forgive but not to forget."

After the speech some of us raised our hands because we had always longed for the day when the President would arrive so we could present our case. He didn't even listen or take a question. The Minister of Defence and Solomon Hawala were there. He just turned and left—showing no interest in listening to us.

Moses Gaoreb, at the time the Administrative Secretary of SWAPO, visited the camps on several occasions. According to an ex-detainee present when Gaoreb came in January 1989:

The fourth and last visit occurred on January 10, 1989, by Moses Gaoreb, the Administrative Secretary of SWAPO. He came to give us a message: "The Central Committee of SWAPO has taken a decision to release you, but with a serious warning. If you happen to resort to your activities against the struggle, there will be no pardoning you next time—you will be executed."

Someone spoke on that occasion and asked for assurances against bodily harm and torture.

The response was: "Consider what you have done regarding the revolution. You will carry this stigma for the rest of your lives. Many have lost their lives because of your collaboration with the enemy. However, as a responsible organization we will give you your protection."

THE HAWALA APPOINTMENT

In October 1990, the government of the Republic of Namibia announced the appointment of Solomon Hawala as Commander of the Army, the third highest position in the Namibian military. The appointment, unlike those of former South African officials, provoked a major controversy.

The Executive Committee of the Council of Churches in Namibia (CCN), which had defended human rights during South African colonial rule, urged the government to "shelve" the appointment until a study of wartime abuses by both sides could be undertaken.[7]

Hawala's appointment was also criticized by Amnesty International, which appealed to the government to set up an impartial inquiry into the alleged torture and killings of political prisoners in the past. Amnesty said: "At the very least, the government should ensure that those responsible are not placed in positions where they could control or have authority over security issues."[8]

---

[7] Press release, October 25, 1990, of the Executive Committee of the Council of Churches in Namibia.

[8] Amnesty International, *Weekly Update*, October 30, 1990.

In a letter to President Nujoma, the Washington D.C.-based Lawyers' Committee for Civil Rights Under Law, an effective monitor of human rights in Namibia, stated:

In our opinion, Mr. Hawala's appointment, and its attendant implications, raises serious human rights as well as moral and political questions. It is for Namibians and their leaders to address the latter issues. But the former issue is of concern to persons everywhere, for this is a matter of the consonance of state actions with international legal standards governing the protection of human rights.[9]

The group called on President Nujoma to reconsider the appointment.

The government and SWAPO strongly defended the appointment. Both the Prime Minister and the Minister of Information accused critics of "selective morality" in "singling" out Hawala. They noted the silence around the retention in the Namibian army and police of officials from the South African forces suspected of abuses during the war. They claimed that these appointments were made pursuant to a government policy of foregoing punishment of ex-soldiers and officials to foster national reconciliation.[10]

An editorial in the official SWAPO newspaper, *Namibia Today*, stated that the only alternative to this policy of national reconciliation was to call for "mass purge, Nuremberg-type of trial and consequent retribution." To single out only one person for human rights abuses, the editorial continued, would be "an exercise in hypocrisy and opportunism."[11] The government was obligated to appoint Hawala, the editorial implied, because the 1982 Constitutional Principles added to Resolution 435 required that it retain former South African colonial officials. There was, however, no legal requirement to retain South African officials credibly associated with abusive practices in their posts. Article 116 of the Constitution empowered the new Inspector-General of Police "to make suitable appointments to the police force." While Article 141 contained a presumption in favor of continued service, it allowed for the retirement, transfer and removal of public employees "in accordance with law." In reply to the *Namibia Today* editorial the General Secretary of the CCN, Abisai Shejavali, said that:

The Namibian constitution does not oblige the government to appoint persons who are allegedly notorious human rights violators . . . . We are in no way calling for

---

[9] Letter to His Excellency President Sam Nujoma, December 3, 1990, the Southern Africa Project of the Lawyers' Committee for Civil Rights under Law.

[10] "Pack and Go, critics of 'Jesus' are told," and "Hamutenya defends 'Jesus' and slams critics," *The Namibian*, October 25, 1990.

[11] "Pack and Go," *The Namibian*, October 25, 1990.

a "Nuremberg type of trial." Our point is that it is not wise to entrust the security of independent and democratic Namibia to persons who have allegedly violated human rights on a gross scale.[12]

SWAPO responded by saying that as the ruling party it would not pay heed to what it considered to be an unacceptable demand: that those who fought for the liberation of the country be "humiliated, harassed, and prevented from their deserved positions in the Namibian government."[13] Citing the policy of national reconciliation, SWAPO contended that:

> we could have chosen to rule alone and to persecute all those who collaborated with the colonialists, particularly those well-known killers and assassins who are responsible for thousands of massacres, disappearances, detentions and tortures of innocent people who are now serving in high positions in the SWAPO government.

SWAPO claimed that the opposition to the Hawala appointment was part of a well-orchestrated campaign aimed at denigrating SWAPO. It further justified the appointment by citing Hawala's wartime experience and his contribution to the liberation struggle.

The Hawala appointment went forward.

---

[12] Ibid.

[13] Ibid.

11. INVESTIGATIONS AFTER INDEPENDENCE

After Namibia gained independence in March 1990, the detainee question became a focus of debate in the National Assembly. Prime Minister Hage Geingob conducted a round of private meetings with political leaders, church organizations, human rights groups and representatives of the former detainees seeking consensus for an inquiry to investigate the fate of all those who had disappeared in detention.[1] On June 1, 1990, Geingob announced that after consulting with other parties, he had accepted a proposal to establish a special committee to resolve the question of those Namibians who had disappeared while in the custody of both sides. This proposal was made by the Minister of Information, Hidipo Hamutenya, as a counter-proposal to a formal motion brought by an opposition party leader, Moses Katjiuongua. The latter's motion had called for establishment of a Judicial Commission of Inquiry. Hamutenya stated that the all-party committee should request the assistance of the International Committee of the Red Cross (ICRC) to investigate the fate of all those disappeared.[2] In the debate over Katjiuongua's motion, Moses Garoeb, who had become SWAPO's Secretary General, denied allegations that the party continued to detain Namibians in camps located outside the country and said that SWAPO itself was compiling a list of all Namibians who disappeared or died during the war. This task was made difficult, he said, by the large number of unmarked graves left by South African forces inside and outside the country.

On July 4, 1990, Prime Minister Geingob met with opposition parties to establish the all-party committee but ceased his efforts when the substance of the discussion was leaked to the opposition press. Months later, on November 9, 1990, the National Assembly passed a resolution calling on Namibia's Chief Justice, Hans Berker, to approach the representative of the ICRC in Windhoek to request that the organization investigate the status of those who had disappeared during the war and were still unaccounted for.[3] In a Memorandum dated December 6, 1990, the ICRC Head of Delegation in Windhoek conveyed the ICRC response. First, according to Chief Justice Berker, because of its mandate, the ICRC could "only deal with the government of a country, and not with a separate branch of it like the National Assembly."[4] Though the ICRC was prepared to assist, it would do so only if the government of the Republic of Namibia submitted a formal request to the organization.

The ICRC set forth several other conditions. It would "initially take up with the parties concerned only unresolved cases which have already been submitted to it." It would then decide on the basis of the results achieved whether it would "be able to deal with new requests from

---

[1] Namibia Communications Centre, "Multi-Party Committee For Missing Namibians," *Namibia Report*, vol. 1, Issue 6, July 1990, p. 2.

[2] Ibid.

[3] "ICRC spells out its conditions on probe," *The Namibian*, April 23, 1991, p. 3. It must be noted that as late as 1989, the ICRC had requested permission from SWAPO to visit the detainees it was holding but SWAPO consistently refused.

[4] "ICRC spells out its conditions on probe," *The Namibian*, April 23, 1991, p. 3.

families that have not yet approached it." If so, it would make a public announcement and inform families how to contact the ICRC.[5]

The Memorandum also stated that: "The spirit of international humanitarian law requires the parties to a conflict to furnish any information they may have on missing persons to those persons' families." To facilitate the ICRC's work, each Namibian political party was asked to designate one of its members to work with the ICRC. It also urged that the National Assembly's motion "encourage any of the foreign governments involved to facilitate the ICRC's tracing work," and suggested that the Namibian government send a copy of the motion to the governments concerned. In those cases where the ICRC learns that a missing person has died, according to the Memorandum, "The circumstances of the death are not necessarily of concern to the ICRC." Finally, the ICRC stated that it "reserves the right at any time to suspend or even cease its tracing work altogether if factors beyond its control prevent it from discharging its mandate under international humanitarian law and the principles of the International Red Cross and Red Crescent Movement."[6] The effect of the Memorandum was to place the burden on the National Assembly to pass another motion instructing the Namibian government to request the ICRC to trace the disappeared.[7]

Nothing happened for several months. Moses Katjiuongua tried to break the deadlock by reintroducing his motion to establish a Judicial Commission of Inquiry and, in April 1991, the question was again taken up by the National Assembly. On April 19, 1991, Mose Tjitendero, the National Assembly Speaker, finally reported to the legislative body that the ICRC would undertake an investigation only if requested by the Namibian government, not by the National Assembly.[8]

The prospect of an ICRC investigation generated criticism. According to a press statement by the Political Consultative Committee, an organization of ex-SWAPO detainees, it was SWAPO's task alone to determine the whereabouts of those reportedly detained by the movement; this responsibility could not be undertaken by the ICRC. The Political Consultative Committee accused the National Assembly of knowingly ignoring ICRC procedures and claimed that the Assembly's November 1990 motion was being used as a "deliberate delaying tactic" by SWAPO.[9]

---

[5] ICRC, Memorandum Re The ICRC and Missing Persons—Motion of the Namibian National Assembly of 9 November 1990.

[6] Ibid.

[7] *Times of Namibia*, "Detainee question tabled in NA," April 22, 1991, p. 1.

[8] *The Namibian*, "NA accused of 'deliberately delaying' detainee question," April 23, 1991, p. 3.

[9] Ibid.

In May 1991, the National Assembly debated Katjiuongua's motion to establish a Judicial Commission of Inquiry headed by a Namibian judge. Katjiuongua categorically stated that the ICRC was not the "appropriate instrument to investigate the matter. It can help in some respects, but not all," he said.[10] His proposal sparked a bitter debate marked by accusations and counter-accusations. Moses Garoeb questioned the "sudden" concern of those who were on the "other side of the liberation struggle." The objective of the motion, according to Garoeb, was "to crucify" SWAPO. He asked if the opposition was calling for Nuremberg-type trials in Namibia and claimed that such trials would damage the policy of national reconciliation by opening old wounds.[11] Other SWAPO legislators reportedly said that the hands of opposition party members were smeared with the blood of innocent Namibians. According to Haduna Hishongwa, a SWAPO delegate, "if there were to be any investigation then it should only be to determine who the real 'war criminals were.'"[12] The Namibian people had demanded that the Government put on trial those who collaborated with the South African government, he said, but it had not done so. Hishongwa said that SWAPO would never allow itself to be put on trial and claimed that the party was the only liberation movement that had detained spies, kept them safely and returned them home. The leader of the official opposition party, the Democratic Turnhalle Alliance (DTA), was described in the swirl of debate as a "killer" and a "war criminal." Finally, SWAPO members walked out of the Assembly.

On May 28, 1991, the National Assembly voted to reject Katjiuongua's motion for the establishment of a Judicial Commission of Inquiry. In response, Katjiuongua said that any amendments to his motion or a new motion would "have the effect of killing the proper investigation of all aspects surrounding the detainee issue through the back door. A watered down, even doctored motion . . . is totally unacceptable to [my party] and me."[13]

On May 29, Namibian Attorney General Hartmut Ruppel said that he would introduce into the National Assembly a motion asking the government to request the ICRC to take up an investigation of the issue of the missing Namibians.[14] Ruppel's motion asked the National Assembly to request the Prime Minister to inform the ICRC of the government's acceptance of its working procedures. Also, it asked the "Prime Minister to request quarterly reports" and called on him to inform the Assembly of the investigation's progress whenever the ICRC submitted such reports. The Prime Minister was also asked to convey the Assembly's resolution

---

[10] "Who's investigating who Swapo NA members ask," *The Namibian*, May 22, 1991, p. 5

[11] "Who's investigating who Swapo NA members ask," May 22, 1991, *The Namibian*, p. 5.

[12] "Exit Swapo: Ruling party walks out of Assembly," *The Namibian*, May 22, 1991, p. 1.

[13] "No vote on detainees," *Times of Namibia*, May 29, 1991, p. 1.

[14] "Detainee deadlock," *The Namibian*, May 30, 1991.

to any foreign government approached by the ICRC during its investigation.[15] On May 31, Ruppel's motion was adopted unanimously by the National Assembly "reiterating the Assembly's continued concern for the right of families to know the fate of their relatives."[16] In June, Prime Minister Geingob sent a letter to the ICRC assuring the organization of the government's full support and of its cooperation in dealing with other governments which may become involved.[17] Accordingly, after a year of maneuvering, in June 1991 the Assembly requested that the government ask the International Committee of the Red Cross to carry out an investigation concerning the disappeared.

While an investigation by the ICRC could provide information about the fate of the missing, it could not address the issue of accountability for the abuses. As a humanitarian organization, the ICRC is not mandated to make determinations about culpability. According to the organization, its tracing work is concerned with:

> obtaining, registering, collating and when necessary forwarding information about people helped by the ICRC; re-establishing contact between separated family members; tracing persons reported missing or whose relatives are without news; drawing up death certificates.[18]

The terms of the ICRC's mandate ensured that its efforts would not deal with the causes, the responsibility or even the more detailed circumstances of those who disappeared.

The ICRC's investigation proceeded slowly during the second half of 1991. Cooperation from the neighboring governments contacted by the Namibian Foreign Ministry was not forthcoming. In November 1991, Nicholas de Rougemont, the ICRC Head of Delegation, noted the lack of support from foreign governments. According to Mr. de Rougemont, initially only SWAPO and the government of Angola had agreed to cooperate in the ICRC tracing mission.[19] De Rougemont said that the ICRC delegations in South Africa, Zambia and Botswana would make follow up requests with those governments. ICRC access to prisons in Angola had led to the return of up to a dozen Namibians at the beginning of November. They were discovered at the Berntiaba (formerly the São Nicolão) Penal Colony north of Port Namibe.

The lack of governmental cooperation was highlighted in the first quarterly report submitted by the ICRC on January 20, 1992. The submission of quarterly progress reports was

---

[15] Ibid.

[16] "Detainee motion accepted," *Times of Namibia*, June 3, 1991.

[17] "Green light for ICRC probe," *The Namibian*, June 24, 1991.

[18] International Committee of the Red Cross, *Annual Report*, 1989, p. 8.

[19] *The Namibian*, November 22, 1991.

required by the terms of the ICRC's arrangement with the Namibian government. In the report the ICRC Head of Delegation indicated that in August 1991, the Foreign Ministry had asked Botswana, Angola, Zambia and South Africa to cooperate. He noted that SWAPO had appointed a liaison officer, Thomas Nekomba, to handle the tracing requests. At that time the ICRC had forwarded seventy tracing requests to Mr. Nekomba but had not received any information on these. According to De Rougemont, "It becomes increasingly likely that our search will lead to graves."[20]

In late January 1992, the ICRC announced that it would close its Delegation by the end of June. Nicolas de Rougemont indicated that the ICRC's peacetime duties would be taken over by the Namibian Red Cross while its protection activities would become the responsibility of the ICRC staff in a nearby state.[21] There was some concern that the ICRC's tracing of detainees would be adversely affected, if not effectively halted, once the Delegation office in Windhoek closed. *The Namibian* reported that there was some feeling that elements within the government were fostering delays in the hope that everything would ground to a halt after the departure of the ICRC.[22] Despite the best efforts of the ICRC staff based in neighboring states, the distance could only the tracing work more difficult.

In February 1992, SWAPO provided its first replies to the ICRC's tracing requests. The ICRC received responses on 28 requests out of several hundred cases submitted to SWAPO over the previous months.[23] According to de Rougemont, the replies contained "enough information to work on." These were all cases of individuals who were "last seen in detention," the designation for SWAPO detainees. The party, however, did not acknowledge their status as detainees.

On April 6, three months prior to the closure of the Delegation office, de Rougemont held a press conference in Windhoek in which he appealed to families with missing relatives to come forward and submit cases not previously registered. As a result of this public appeal, the ICRC received 1,710 new tracing requests in the following eight weeks. According to de Rougemont, the ICRC was receiving new cases every day. The ICRC had sent 1,200 cases to SWAPO and was planning to forward the remaining 510 before June 30. The ICRC had received 170 replies. Most of these new cases concerned missing PLAN fighters; roughly 90% of those were reported to have died in combat as PLAN fighters. Thirty who were reported as having been "last seen in detention" were reported by SWAPO to have died of disease in Angola, a tacit admission that they died in SWAPO custody.

---

[20] *Southscan*, January 24, 1992.

[21] *The Namibian*, January 23, 1992.

[22] Ibid.

[23] *The Namibian*, February 19, 1992.

The SWAPO liaison, Thomas Nekomba, reported that most of the cases fit into three categories: those who died fighting; those who died in the settlements from illness or accidents; and those who died while studying abroad. He added that the most difficult cases concerned those who went missing. According to Nekomba, these were people who went missing in southern Angola while travelling between bases and in the war zone. It was not clear he said, whether they had been killed or captured by South African troops or possibly detained by UNITA forces.[24]

The massive response to the ICRC public appeal suggests the scope of the problem of the disappeared. While the majority of the 1,700 cases apparently did not involve SWAPO detainees, these 1,700 only included cases received in writing by the ICRC from relatives. They do not necessarily include the hundreds of names of detainees on lists prepared by former detainees and other groups.

The outpouring also suggests that many people had held back. It highlighted that neither PLAN nor SWAPO ever notified the families of the fate of the missing. While many families knew that their relatives had died, they had never received written confirmation of their status. Effectively, by transmitting this information the ICRC is doing SWAPO/PLAN's work.

On May 12, the ICRC submitted its second quarterly report on the progress in its tracing work to Prime Minister Hage Geingob. In June, President Frederick Chiluba of Zambia indicated that his government would cooperate with the ICRC's tracing efforts. Since Botswana had responded positively earlier in the year, only South Africa had refused consent.

Though the ICRC's tracing work has provided information about the ultimate fate of a number of the missing, Africa Watch believes that accountability for disappearances in the transition to democracy in Namibia remains an open question that should be addressed by the governments of Namibia, Angola and South Africa.

---

[24] Graham Hopwood, "Flood of missing persons requests," *The Namibian*, May 27, 1992.

RECOMMENDATIONS

In light of the serious abuses documented in this report by the forces of the South African colonial regime and the SWAPO security services, Africa Watch is making the following recommendations in order to facilitate accountability for those abuses:

The South African government should:

* Establish a Commission of stature and independence to disclose and acknowledge the abusive practices of its forces during the struggle for independence in Namibia.

* Provide all reliable information about disappearances and deaths, including information about individuals captured and/or killed in Angola.

* Open its files to such a Commission for examination.

* Withdraw the appointment of any official credibly linked to serious human rights abuses.

The Namibian government should:

* Establish a "Truth Commission" of stature and independence to account for all those who disappeared. Such a Commission would identify those missing; state what is known about their detention and the circumstances of their disappearance; and identify those responsible for the disappearance.

* Withdraw the appointment of those who have been credibly associated with serious human rights abuses.

Furthermore, President Sam Nujoma and other members of the SWAPO leadership should:

* State publicly for the record their knowledge of the conditions and treatment of the detainees, including the details of their visits to the camps; and the policies behind the arrests and detentions.

The Angolan government should:

* Provide all useful and credible information on detainees not released by SWAPO.

* Provide all information in its records about the detention facility maintained by SWAPO in Angola.

* Provide information about any Namibians still in its custody.

* Open its official files to a Namibian Commission.

The United States government should:

    * Use its influence to encourage the parties involved to contribute to the accounting for abuses.

The United Nations should:

    * Open the files of the United Nations Transition Assistance Group concerning the release of detainees from camps in Angola.

APPENDIX 1
Human Rights Watch Policy on Accountability for Past Abuses—1988

Human Rights Watch holds that those who commit gross abuses of human rights should be held accountable for their crimes. It is a responsibility of governments to seek accountability regardless of whether the perpetrators of such abuses are officials of the government itself and its armed forces, or officials of a predecessor government, or members of anti-government forces, or others. We oppose laws and practices that purport to immunize those who have committed gross abuses from the exposure of their crimes, from civil suits for damages for those crimes, or from criminal investigation, prosecution and punishment.

Human Rights Watch recognizes the difficulty that some governments may face in holding members of their own armed forces accountable for their gross abuses of human rights. Also, we recognize that military regimes may insist, explicitly or implicitly, on immunity from accountability as a condition for relinquishing their offices and permitting the establishment of elected civilian governments. We do not believe that these difficulties justify disregard for the principle of accountability. We consider that accountability for gross abuses should remain a goal of a government that seeks to promote respect for human rights.

In pursuing that goal, Human Rights Watch holds:

☐ that the most important means of establishing accountability is for the government itself to make known all that can be reliably established about gross abuses of human rights; their nature and extent; the identities of the victims; the identities of those responsible for devising the policies and practices that resulted in gross abuses; the identities of those who carried out gross abuses; and the identities of those who knowingly aided and abetted those who carried out gross abuses;

☐ that laws and decrees purporting to immunize the perpetrators of gross abuses from accountability are null and void: (a) when promulgated by the perpetrators themselves; (b) when applied to crimes against humanity; or (c) when otherwise in conflict with international law;

☐ that the duty to investigate, prosecute and punish those responsible for gross abuses is proportionate to the extent and severity of the abuses and the degree of responsibility for such abuses. Accordingly, though we advocate criminal prosecution and punishment for those who have the highest degree of responsibility for the most severe abuses of human rights, we recognize that accountability may be achieved by public disclosure and condemnation in cases of lesser responsibility and/or less severe abuses. The determination of who should be prosecuted will have to be made according to the circumstances of each situation. In making such determinations, we believe it is essential that there should be no granting of impunity either because of the identity of those responsible for gross abuses of human rights or because of the identity of the victims;

☐   that popular disinclination to hold accountable those responsible for gross abuses does not negate the responsibility of a government to pursue accountability, particularly in circumstances where the victims of abuses may have been concentrated among members of a racial, ethnic, religious or political minority. A government's duty to demonstrate respect for human rights extends to all persons, and it is not the prerogative of the many to forgive the commission of crimes against the few;

☐   that laws, decrees and practices that immunize members of the armed forces from accountability do not enjoy any greater validity because of a purported symmetry with amnesties for anti-government forces. Though amnesties for crimes of opposition to the state and the established political order, including by means of armed combat, may be justified as a means of persuading members of anti-government forces to lay down their arms, we oppose their extension to those within such forces who have committed gross abuses of human rights;

☐   that obedience to orders (in circumstances other than duress) is not a valid defense to charges of responsibility for gross abuses of human rights. To the extent that obedience to orders is relevant to prosecutions, it should be only as a mitigating circumstance that may be considered by judges according to the facts of each case in determining the appropriate punishment;

☐   that the means employed by a government in making known what can be reliably established about gross abuses, and in investigating, prosecuting and punishing those responsible, should at all times conform to internationally recognized principles of due process of law.

Human Rights Watch believes that nongovernmental human rights can themselves make a valuable contribution in securing accountability for gross abuses by insisting that a government's policies on these matters should be publicly debated; by gathering evidence on gross abuses for submission to the government; and, in circumstances when a government has not fulfilled (or not yet fulfilled) its duty to hold accountable those responsible for gross abuses, by gathering and publishing their own carefully documented accounts.

Human Rights Watch will pursue such opportunities as may be available to strengthen the commitment to accountability in international law; will attempt to use the machinery of international law in appropriate cases to secure accountability; and will aid domestic human rights groups in other countries in securing accountability in accordance with the policies stated above.

As used here, the term gross abuses of human rights applies to:

* genocide;
* arbitrary, summary or extrajudicial executions;
* forced or involuntary disappearances;

* torture or other gross physical abuses;
* prolonged arbitrary deprivation of liberty.